SELECTED POEMS I

David Wheatley teaches modern lite⟨…⟩ ⟨…⟩ ⟨…⟩ ⟨…⟩ ⟨…⟩ University of
Hull. He has published three collections of poetry with
Gallery Press.

SAMUEL BECKETT

Selected Poems
1930–1989
Edited by David Wheatley

faber and faber

Collected Poems in English and French
published in 1977 by John Calder, London

This edition first published in 2009
by Faber and Faber Ltd
Bloomsbury House
74–77 Great Russell Street
London WC1B 3DA

Typeset byRefineCatch Limited, Bungay, Suffolk
Printed in England by CPI Bookmarque, Croydon

A CIP record for this book
is available from the British Library

ISBN 978–0–571–24372–3

2 4 6 8 10 9 7 5 3 1

Contents

[Note: *Echo's Bones* was Beckett's only separately published collection of poems, but as the French poems of the 1930s and 1940s and the *mirlitonnades* all form sequences in their own right, all three are marked as such in the Contents.]

Preface

Samuel Beckett began and ended his career with poetry. From *Whoroscope* (1930) to 'what is the word' (1989) is a lifetime's arc of writing. It was as a poet that the young Beckett launched himself in the little reviews of 1930s Paris, and as a poet that he would make his first breakthrough into writing in French. From the outset poetry was central to Beckett's work, from the abject majesty of the Leopardi epigraph to his book on Proust (*'E fango è il mondo'*; 'and the world is mud') to his lifelong engagement with Dante, Racine, Keats, Hölderlin and other favourites. 'The poem of poems', Beckett wrote in 'Recent Irish Poetry', 'would embrace the sense of confinement, the getaway, the vicissitudes of the road, the wan bliss on the rim', and even allowing for the critical tone here (Beckett is deprecating his Irish contemporaries), an oscillation between contrary states is a defining condition of his own work too. Beckett the poet alternates between expansiveness and concision, slapstick humour and Zen-like calm, claustrophobic trampings round Dublin and moments of blissful centrifugal escape. Escape not just from Ireland but the larger Anglosphere was a deeply felt need: Beckett translated Rimbaud, Éluard and Apollinaire and served his time in the trench wars of Irish poetic modernism, forswearing Yeats but embracing neither Eliot's Christianity nor the emerging idiolect of Auden, MacNeice and Spender. 'Keep on the move,' Beckett writes at the end of 'Serena III', and it was a stylistic principle to which his poetry would cleave assiduously. Though his ambitions quickly overspilled any one genre, Beckett's plays and fiction are also full of poetry, from the polyglot doodles of *Dream of Fair to Middling Women* and the nonsense rhymes of *Watt* to Hamm's intoning of Baudelaire in

Endgame and the dramatised versification of *Words and Music*. Beckett's work as a whole has never wanted for exegetes, but the poems remain a somewhat mandarin interest, attracting a band of advocates that has nevertheless included Michael Hamburger, Thomas Kinsella and Derek Mahon, while among composers György Kurtág, Morton Feldman and Marcel Mihalovici have all responded with musical settings.

Traditionally the *Incipit* of the Beckett canon, 'Whoroscope' was composed in 1930 as a last-minute entry for a poetry competition on the subject of time. The poem is spoken by Descartes, who has been employed by Queen Christina of Sweden to teach her philosophy; unfortunately for him, as a life-long late riser, the classes are at dawn. Hence perhaps the abandonment of cool reasoning on the mind-body divide for the absurdist theatrics of Descartes sitting in the hot-cupboard 'throwing Jesuits out of the skylight'. The notes Beckett appends to the poem exploit the new-found freedoms of *The Waste Land* while simultaneously sidestepping Eliotian solemnity ('In 1640 the brothers Boot refuted Aristotle in Dublin'). A reference to Augustine proving God 'by exhaustion' provides an early example of 'the loutishness of learning' (in the words of 'Gnome'), contorting the unobliging universe into patterns of reasonableness and sense. Derek Mahon, otherwise one of Beckett's strongest admirers, finds the poem's parade of learning altogether too loutish. However, if 'Whoroscope' must finally be judged (in its own words) the 'abortion of a fledgling', it sets a tone of what *Murphy* calls 'eleutheromania', or rage for freedom, that Beckett will follow in his later poems and their more successful puncturing of the embryos of callow youth.

The young Beckett's keenness to emulate Joyce extended to wearing the tight-fitting, pigeon-toed shoes favoured by the older man; and to contemplate the punning style of 'Home Olga', an acrostic tribute to Joyce not included here, is to witness Beckett shoehorn himself into a style patently not his. The juvenilia published by Beckett in the 1930s secrete allusions like cuttlefish ink, behind which lurks a spluttering and inchoate poetic ego. The baroque glory of titles such as 'From the Only Poet to a Shining Whore' and 'Casket of Pralinen for a Daughter of a Dissipated Mandarin' is among the most striking things about these poems, which are probably best read in tandem with the exhaustive commentaries in Lawrence Harvey's 1970 study, *Samuel Beckett: Poet and Critic*.

A striking albeit exiled exception among the juvenilia is 'Yoke of Liberty' (originally 'Moly'), whose ceremonial vocabulary ('torn', 'grave', 'watchful', 'pitiful') links it to 'Alba' and 'Dortmunder' which were included in *Echo's Bones*, published in 1935 by George Reavey's Europa Press in Paris. From the biblical exhortation to 'the prone' in the opening poem, 'The Vulture', that they 'take up their life and walk', the volume's thirteen poems embark on a variety of journeys that, variously, go nowhere or reveal themselves as preludes to the funeral procession of 'Malacoda', written in deep grief for Beckett's father, who died in 1933 ('all aboard all souls / half-mast aye aye / nay'). While Beckett refused to authorise a reprint of *More Pricks than Kicks* until 1970, he was happy in later life to keep the poems of *Echo's Bones* in print; to Hugh Kenner, they seemed the only part of his early work for which Beckett still cared. At the time, though, the book passed almost without notice: 'five lines of faint damn in *Dublin Mag*', as Beckett lamented to Thomas MacGreevy, with the added insult that many of Beckett's friends, already familiar with the poems, refused to buy copies. 'Getting known', as Krapp declared, contemplating his 'seventeen copies sold'.

Beckett's hopes for *Echo's Bones* must have extended beyond a favourable review in the *Dublin Magazine*, but despite resigning from his teaching post at Trinity he still found himself, in the mid-1930s, more embroiled in Dublin literary life than can have been comfortable. His prose had so far failed to put the necessary distance between him and the hated *littérateurs* of Dublin pub life: *Dream of Fair to Middling Women* had been abandoned, *More Pricks Than Kicks* banned, and *Murphy* would endure dozens of rejections before its publication in 1938. The inducements to a little local score-settling were strong, and in 'Recent Irish Poetry', writing as 'Andrew Belis', Beckett launched a rollicking denunciation of his contemporaries. His prime targets are the 'antiquarians' still wedded to Gaelic revivalism in the age of modernist 'rupture of the lines of communication'. These include F. R. Higgins and Austin Clarke, soon to be pilloried as the hapless 'Austin Ticklepenny' of *Murphy*. The young Beckett was not one for nuance on the subject of Ireland and Irish poetry in the 1930s, and kept his raids on mythology studiously free of the Celtic 'fully licensed stock-in-trade' beloved of Higgins and Clarke. Though always an admirer of Jack Yeats, as both painter and novelist, Beckett also resisted the poetry of W. B. Yeats; evidence of his belated conversion to its merits can be found in Anne Atik's memoir *How It Was*.

The unpublished essay 'Censorship in the Saorstat' links Irish anti-intellectualism and sexual Puritanism. Sex is everywhere and nowhere in 1930s Ireland: writing to MacGreevy in 1931 Beckett complains of Seumas O'Sullivan sizing up his submissions to the *Dublin Magazine* for obscene anagrams. Erotic thoughts in the early poems lead to wallowing abjection ('girls taken strippin that's the idea') or hopeless sublimation. 'Sanies II' remembers Becky Cooper's brothel in Dublin's Railway Street (whither Belacqua makes his way at the end of the short story 'Ding-Dong'); the print of Henry Holiday's 'Dante and Beatrice' on the wall shows what fertile ground the Beckett narrator finds in these 'sites of rendezvous' for the Madonna-whore complex expounded in *Dream of Fair to Middling Women*. The French title used for a 1967 gathering of short prose, *Têtes-mortes*, refers to the leftovers from a process of alchemical sublimation, and in 'Alba' an ethereal woman bestows her grace from on high but utterly fails to ennoble the base metal of the Beckettian ego, or raise him up to her level. Where other poems from *Echo's Bones* rage hysterically against this impasse, 'Alba' achieves an oriental calm, with its lute music, silk and bamboo, suggesting careful study of Pound's 'Cathay' and the contemporary translations of Arthur Waley:

before morning you shall be here
and Dante and the Logos and all strata and mysteries
and the branded moon
beyond the white plane of music
that you shall establish here before morning

Several of the poems of *Echo's Bones* adopt Provençal titles: a 'Serena' is a lover's song of anticipation, sung at evening, and the 'Alba' the song of the departing lover at dawn; 'Enueg' is the Provençal for 'ennui'. Another gnomic title, 'Sanies', refers to a seropurulent discharge, and not without reason; Beckett's medical history for this period is one long catalogue of skin complaints, as though even at an epidermal level integration into his Irish surroundings was beyond him. The walker of 'Enueg I' launches into his trek round Dublin 'in a spasm', proceeding by a series of cinematic jump-cut transitions that remind us of Beckett's ambition in the mid-1930s to study with Eisenstein in Moscow. 'Enueg I' alternates between social realism and incantation, keen as ever to bundle the self offstage ('the mind annulled /wrecked in wind'), and ending with a quatrain transplanted from Rimbaud's 'Barbare'. A long poem of MacGreevy's from this period, 'Crón Tráth na nDéithe' (the Gaelic, roughly, for *Götterdämmerung*), employs similar tactics of modernist collage and fragmentation, but predicated on an investment in Irish nationalism which is simply lacking in Beckett, for all the rediscovery in recent decades of his previously undervalued Irishness. The poems of *Echo's Bones* are intensely claustrophobic, but while their Irish locales may appear inescapable (just as leaving the city is physically beyond the denizens of Joyce's *Dubliners*), their truest home remains 'unspeakable', in the formulation of the late text 'neither'. The urban peripatetics of *Mercier and Camier* and the post-war novellas, not to mention his kinship with Apollinaire's 'Zone', have their self-shredding roots in poems such as 'Sanies I'.

Robert Lowell found that John Berryman's work operated in a spin-cycle of 'prayer' and 'riot', and Beckett's critical pronouncements offer some perspective on his own wavering between the meditative and the unruly. Of Thomas MacGreevy he wrote in 1934: 'All poetry, as discriminated from the various paradigms of prosody, is prayer.' A review of Denis Devlin four years later makes the obscurantist counter-argument, advancing 'the vile suggestion that art has nothing to do with clarity, does not dabble in the clear and does not make clear'. Beckett's poems in English after *Echo's Bones* continue to thrive on authorial quarrels with the self, from the fulminating blasphemies of 'Ooftish' to the lovelorn cries of 'Cascando'. While the God the Father figure of 'Ooftish' greedily feeds on human suffering ('we'll make use of it /we'll make sense of it'), the disappointed lover of 'Cascando' looks to non-existence instead ('is it not better abort than be barren'). Neither poem uses any punctuation, so when 'Cascando' ponders 'last times [...] /of knowing not knowing pretending', it is tempting to hear 'not knowing' as the Zen-like object of 'knowing', and of the wise passivity towards which Beckett's poetry increasingly gravitates.

1937 saw Beckett make his permanent home in Paris and begin to compose in French, in a sequence of twelve poems published after the war in *Les Temps modernes*. His usual practice after his adoption of French was to produce versions of new texts in both French and English, sometimes, as with *Mercier and Camier*, allowing decades to elapse before completing the task. His poetry is anomalous in this regard, as the bulk of his poems exist in only English or French. In the case of poems such as 'they come'/'*elles viennent*', it is not immediately apparent which, if either, of the two texts should be thought of as the original and which the translation. Depending on one's preference, Beckett has written one poem twice or two poems once. The Spanish edition of Beckett's poems responds to this by translating 'they come' and '*elles viennent*' separately, enacting the poem's theme in a trilingual constellation of sameness and difference.

Esse est percipi, to be is to be perceived, according to Bishop Berkeley but the roles of observer and observed shift constantly in these poems, along with the limits of the unitary self that might underwrite them ('everything divides into itself', as Beckett writes in *Malone Dies*). A reference to Immanuel Kant contemplating the Lisbon earthquake suggests the seismic upsets Beckett has set himself to absorb, and it is hardly a co-incidence that many of these poems end with an image of flight from upheaval and violence. 'Saint-Lô' vibrates to the echoes of a more recent catastrophe, commemorating Beckett's work with the Red Cross in that devastated Normandy town after the war and watching 'the old mind ghost-forsaken /sink into its havoc'. If the self fragments in '*Arènes de Lutèce*', in '*Rue de Vaugirard*' he isolates a fugitive moment in time before peeling the self away from it like a photographic negative ('*un négatif irrécusable*'). Beckett does something similar in the lovely quatrain 'Dieppe', which he skims intertextually from Hölderlin's '*Der Spaziergang*'.

The Unnamable, in the novel of that name, comes to believe that he is a tympanum, 'the thing that divides the world in two', and increasingly the French poems master the turmoil of the earlier work by reaching for a state of quietist in-betweenness:

> my way is in the sand flowing
> between the shingle and the dune
> the summer rain rains on my life
> on me my life harrying fleeing
> to its beginning to its end

The end is in the beginning and yet we go on, though after the mainly French poems of the 1940s Beckett took an extended hiatus from poetry, even if his fiction and plays continued to feature poems (e.g. 'Song', from *Words and Music*). It is a notable feature of Beckett's later work that his fiction and drama begin to take on each other's characteristics (the stage-direction-style arrangement of the bodies in *The Lost Ones* and

Imagination Dead Imagine, the fiction-like *A Piece of Monologue*, the appropriately named 'neither', written as an opera libretto), and by the time we reach his last poems we are dealing with texts that could be in any, or all of his genres.

Many Beckett plays isolate and detach the act of speech, most strikingly in the disembodied mouth of *Not I*, and an element of narrative extortion is an undeniable presence in later Beckett. Another aspect of his later work is the harnessing of speech to carefully choreographed movement, as in 'Roundelay' but also in late plays and prose texts such as *Footfalls* and 'The Way'. Chief among the late poems, however, are the *mirlitonnades*. These are described in an earlier John Calder edition (*Collected Poems 1930–1978* (1984)) as 'written spasmodically on scraps of paper. Nothing dated.' While some of these poems were originally written on café bills and hotel notepaper, this is not the whole story: Beckett carefully copied and arranged the poems in the *mirlitonnades* '*sottisier*' notebook now held by the Beckett International Foundation, University of Reading. If these poems are 'breathtaking glimpses of being and nothingness', as Justin Quinn has called them, they often take less than a breath to read aloud. At a minimum of as few as seven words, they are as carefully weighed as a Webern bagatelle, and come as close as anything Beckett wrote to honouring the ambition outlined in his 1937 letter to Axel Kaun to 'bore one hole after another in [language], until what lurks behind it – be it something or nothing – begins to seep through'. The *mirlitonnades* rank high among Beckett's late achievements, and do much to usher in the style of his late prose narratives (*Company, Ill Seen Ill Said, Worstward Ho*).

Beckett's poetic last word was 'what is the word', translated from the preceding French text '*comment dire*' in the Tiers Temps nursing home in 1989. (The *Faber Companion to Samuel Beckett* reports that the poem was printed from Barbara Bray's computer, Beckett's 'word' processed at last.) And what is the word? the reader may wonder, mentally overstepping the mark and supplying the question mark the poem so noticeably lacks:

>folly –
>folly for to –
>for to –
>what is the word –
>folly from this –
>all this –
>folly from all this –
>given –
>folly given all this –
>seeing –
>folly seeing all this –
>this –
>what is the word –

We can of course collapse the quest for the elusive Logos at any moment by deciding that the word in question is 'what', a suspicion licensed by the omission of the poem's otherwise ubiquitous, jabbing dash, in the final line, as though coming to rest at last: 'what is the word'. With fitting symmetry the French version, '*comment dire*', contradicts any closure this reading threatens to provide by moving in the opposite direction, bogging down further and further away from the word it seeks ('*comment dire – /comment dire*'). Dragged in both directions at once by the English and French texts, we are delivered to a final resting place of precisely nowhere: 'unspeakable home' once more.

Where Beckett's publishing history is concerned, his post-war poetry publications are effectively a series of updated *Collected*s with the unusual distinction of becoming less and less reliable as they go along, the multiply defective *Poems 1930–1989* (2002) marking a low point in the history of Beckett editing. The rationale to the present *Selected* has been to take a fresh look at the poetry without pretending to the scholarly exhaustiveness promised by John Pilling and Seán Lawlor's forthcoming new *Collected Poems in English and French*. Nevertheless, some effort has been made to address the many anomalies that surround

Beckett's uncollected and unpublished work. The *mirlitonnades* *'sottisier'* contains a number of striking short poems, in both French and English, which post-date the publication of that sequence in 1978, and while Beckett made no effort to collect them in book form it would be wrong to see them as rejected by him; rather, they represent a partial further evolution of the sequence. Other marginal zones of the poetic *œuvre* also yield unexpected rewards. Translations represent some of Beckett's finest poetic achievements. His version of Ernst Moerman's 'Louis Armstrong' for the *Negro Anthology* follows to an uncanny degree the poetic grammar of *Echo's Bones*. Beckett the non-self-translator is another matter again, and where his French poems are concerned the *en face* translations are by Beckett alone, with prose versions of poems untranslated by Beckett supplied in an appendix.

Beckett is a writer whose fiction and drama effortlessly attain the condition of poetry, and some of whose great work happens to be in strictly, or not so strictly, poetic form. While his three coevals lauded in 'Recent Irish Poetry' (Thomas MacGreevy, Brian Coffey and Denis Devlin) are often cited as evidence of a shared aesthetic, Beckett's insistence, *contra* nationalist canonisations of Jack Yeats, that 'the artist who stakes his being is from nowhere, has no kith' renders the concept of Irish poetic modernism as a shared front null and void. Beckett's poetry might just as fruitfully be compared to the Objectivist poetics of George Oppen or Lorine Niedecker and the later W. S. Graham. It is also important to keep a sense of French poets such as Éluard, Char and Michaux as no less Beckett's contemporaries, while his early translation of Montale hints at elective affinities further afield too. More recent writers as diverse as Susan Howe, Mahon and Trevor Joyce have also learned from Beckett's poetry; and if this trio of names suggests the Irish context is not as easily disposed of as I may have hinted, there is always *Watt*'s chastening reminder that 'for all the good that frequent departures out of Ireland had done him, he might just as well have stayed there'. Finally, though, admirers of Beckett's poetry find themselves in the peculiar position of wishing to rescue this work from the casual neglect of literary history while having to acknowledge that the deepest instinct of these poems is not to belong, in literary history or anywhere else. Ireland, the home place, any place, the self, language itself: on all Beckett passes the same impartial verdict of 'away dream all /away'. Yet will themselves away as they might, Beckett's poems cannot quite vanish as they go, but secrete themselves in their strange and compelling variety. Or as he writes in *Malone Dies*, 'the forms are many in which the unchanging seeks relief from its formlessness.'

Table of Dates

Where unspecified, translations from French to English or vice versa are by Beckett.

1906

13 April   Samuel Beckett [Samuel Barclay Beckett] born in 'Cooldrinagh', a house in Foxrock, a village south of Dublin, on Good Friday, the second child of William Beckett and May Beckett, née Roe; he is preceded by a brother, Frank Edward, born 26 July 1902.

1911

Enters kindergarten at Ida and Pauline Elsner's private academy in Leopardstown.

1915

Attends larger Earlsfort House School in Dublin.

1920

Follows Frank to Portora Royal, a distinguished Protestant boarding school in Enniskillen, County Fermanagh (soon to become part of Northern Ireland).

1923

October   Enrols at Trinity College Dublin (TCD) to study for an Arts degree.

1926

August   First visit to France, a month-long cycling tour of the Loire Valley.

1927

April–August   Travels through Florence and Venice, visiting museums, galleries, and churches.

December   Receives B.A. in Modern Languages (French and Italian) and graduates first in the First Class.

xxi

1928

Jan.–June — Teaches French and English at Campbell College, Belfast.

September — First trip to Germany to visit seventeen-year-old Peggy Sinclair, a cousin on his father's side, and her family in Kassel.

1 November — Arrives in Paris as an exchange *lecteur* at the École Normale Supérieure. Quickly becomes friends with his predecessor, Thomas McGreevy [after 1943, MacGreevy], who introduces Beckett to James Joyce and other influential anglophone writers and publishers.

December — Spends Christmas in Kassel (as also in 1929, 1930 and 1931).

1929

June — Publishes first critical essay ('Dante . . . Bruno . Vico . . Joyce') and first story ('Assumption') in *transition* magazine.

1930

July — *Whoroscope* (Paris: Hours Press).

October — Returns to TCD to begin a two-year appointment as lecturer in French.

November — Introduced by MacGreevy to the painter and writer Jack B. Yeats in Dublin.

1931

March — *Proust* (London: Chatto and Windus).

September — First Irish publication, the poem 'Alba' in *Dublin Magazine*.

1932

January — Resigns his lectureship via telegram from Kassel and moves to Paris.

Feb.–June — First serious attempt at a novel, the posthumously published *Dream of Fair to Middling Women*.

December — Story 'Dante and the Lobster' appears in *This Quarter* (Paris).

1933

3 May	Death of Peggy Sinclair from tuberculosis.
26 June	Death of William Beckett from a heart attack.

1934

January	Moves to London and begins psychoanalysis with Wilfred Bion at the Tavistock Clinic.
February	*Negro Anthology*, edited by Nancy Cunard and with numerous translations by Beckett from the French (London: Wishart and Company).
May	*More Pricks Than Kicks* (London: Chatto and Windus).
Aug.–Sept.	Contributes several stories and reviews to literary magazines in London and Dublin.

1935

November	*Echo's Bones and Other Precipitates*, a cycle of thirteen poems (Paris: Europa Press).

1936

	Returns to Dublin.
29 September	Leaves Ireland for a seven-month stay in Germany.

1937

Apr.–Aug.	First serious attempt at a play, *Human Wishes*, about Samuel Johnson and his household.
October	Settles in Paris.

1938

6/7 January	Stabbed by a street pimp in Montparnasse. Among his visitors at Hôpital Broussais is Suzanne Deschevaux-Dumesnil, an acquaintance who is to become Beckett's companion for life.
March	*Murphy* (London: Routledge).
April	Begins writing poetry directly in French.

1939

3 September	Great Britain and France declare war on Germany. Beckett abruptly ends a visit to Ireland and returns to Paris the next day.

1950

25 August   Death of May Beckett.

1951

March   *Molloy*, in French (Paris: Les Éditions de Minuit).

November   *Malone meurt* (Paris: Minuit).

1952

Purchases land at Ussy-sur-Marne, subsequently Beckett's preferred location for writing.

September   *En attendant Godot* (Paris: Minuit).

1953

5 January   Premiere of *Godot* at the Théâtre de Babylone in Montparnasse, directed by Roger Blin.

May   *L'Innommable* (Paris: Minuit).

August   *Watt*, in English (Paris: Olympia Press).

1954

8 September   *Waiting for Godot* (New York: Grove Press).

13 September   Death of Frank Beckett from lung cancer.

1955

March   *Molloy*, translated into English with Patrick Bowles (New York: Grove; Paris: Olympia).

3 August   First English production of *Godot* opens in London at the Arts Theatre.

November   *Nouvelles et Textes pour rien* (Paris: Minuit).

1956

3 January   American *Godot* premiere in Miami.

February   First British publication of *Waiting for Godot* (London: Faber).

October   *Malone Dies* (New York: Grove).

1957

January   First radio broadcast, *All That Fall* on the BBC Third Programme.

Fin de partie, suivi de Acte sans paroles (Paris: Minuit).

28 March   Death of Jack B. Yeats.

Court Theatre in honour of Beckett's
seventieth birthday.

Autumn   *All Strange Away*, illustrated with etchings by
Edward Gorey (New York: Gotham Book
Mart).

Foirades/Fizzles, in French and English,
illustrated with etchings by Jasper Johns (New
York: Petersburg Press).

December   *Footfalls* (London: Faber).

1977

March   *Collected Poems in English and French* (London:
Calder; New York: Grove).

1978

May   *Pas*, translation of *Footfalls* (Paris: Minuit).

August   *Poèmes, suivi de mirlitonnades* (Paris: Minuit).

1980

January   *Compagnie* (Paris: Minuit).

Company (London: Calder).

May   Directs *Endgame* in London with Rick
Cluchey and the San Quentin Drama
Workshop.

1981

March   *Mal vu mal dit* (Paris: Minuit).

April   *Rockaby and Other Short Pieces* (New York:
Grove).

October   *Ill Seen Ill Said*, translation of *Mal vu mal dit*
(New York: *New Yorker*; Grove).

1983

April   *Worstward Ho* (London: Calder).

September   *Disjecta: Miscellaneous Writings and a
Dramatic Fragment*, containing critical
essays on art and literature as well as the
unfinished play *Human Wishes*
(London: Calder).

1984

February   Oversees San Quentin Drama Workshop

production of *Godot*, directed by Walter
Asmus, in London.

Collected Shorter Plays (London: Faber; New
York: Grove).

May — *Collected Poems 1930–1978* (London: Calder).

July — *Collected Shorter Prose 1945–1980* (London:
Calder).

1989

April — *Stirrings Still*, with illustrations by Louis le
Brocquy (New York: Blue Moon Books).

June — *Nohow On: Company, Ill Seen Ill Said, Worstward
Ho*, illustrated with etchings by Robert Ryman
(New York: Limited Editions Club).

17 July — Death of Suzanne Beckett.

22 December — Death of Samuel Beckett. Burial in Cimetière
de Montparnasse.

★

1990

*As the Story Was Told: Uncollected and Late
Prose* (London: Calder; New York: Riverrun
Press).

1992

Dream of Fair to Middling Women (Dublin:
Black Cat Press).

1995

Eleutheria (Paris: Minuit).

1996

Eleutheria, translated into English by Barbara
Wright (London: Faber).

1998

*No Author Better Served: The Correspondence of
Samuel Beckett and Alan Schneider*, edited by
Maurice Harmon (Cambridge MA: Harvard
University Press).

2000

Beckett on Film: nineteen films, by different directors, of Beckett's works for the stage (RTÉ, Channel 4, and Irish Film Board; DVD, London: Clarence Pictures).

2006

Samuel Beckett: Works for Radio: The Original Broadcasts: five works spanning the period 1957–1976 (CD, London: British Library Board).

2009

The Letters of Samuel Beckett 1929–1940, edited by Martha Dow Fehsenfeld and Lois More Overbeck (Cambridge: Cambridge University Press).

Compiled by Cassandra Nelson

Draft of poem from *mirlitonnades*
Courtesy of the Beckett International Foundation, University of Reading.
© The Estate of Samuel Beckett.

Selected Poems 1930–1989

Whoroscope

What's that?
An egg?
By the brothers Boot it stinks fresh.
Give it to Gillot.

Galileo how are you
and his consecutive thirds!
The vile old Copernican lead-swinging son of a sutler!
We're moving he said we're off – Porca Madonna!
the way a boatswain would be, or a sack-of-potatoey
   charging Pretender.
That's not moving, that's *moving*.   10

What's that?
A little green fry or a mushroomy one?
Two lashed ovaries with prostisciutto?
How long did she womb it, the feathery one?
Three days and four nights?
Give it to Gillot.

Faulhaber, Beeckman and Peter the Red,
come now in the cloudy avalanche or Gassendi's sun-red
   crystally cloud
and I'll pebble you all your hen-and-a-half ones
or I'll pebble a lens under the quilt in the midst of day.   20

3

To think he was my own brother, Peter the Bruiser,
and not a syllogism out of him
no more than if Pa were still in it.
Hey! pass over those coppers,
sweet millèd sweat of my burning liver!
Them were the days I sat in the hot-cupboard throwing
    Jesuits out of the skylight.

Who's that? Hals?
Let him wait.

My squinty doaty!
I hid and you sook.   30
And Francine my precious fruit of a house-and-parlour
    foetus!
What an exfoliation!
Her little grey flayed epidermis and scarlet tonsils!
My one child
scourged by a fever to stagnant murky blood –
blood!
Oh Harvey belovèd
how shall the red and white, the many in the few,
(dear bloodswirling Harvey)
eddy through that cracked beater?   40
And the fourth Henry came to the crypt of the arrow.

What's that?
How long?
Sit on it.

4

A wind of evil flung my despair of ease
against the sharp spires of the one
lady:
not once or twice but. . . .
(Kip of Christ hatch it!)
in one sun's drowning   50
(Jesuitasters please copy).
So on with the silk hose over the knitted, and the morbid
    leather –
what am I saying! the gentle canvas –
and away to Ancona on the bright Adriatic,
and farewell for a space to the yellow key of the
    Rosicrucians.
They don't know what the master of them that do did,
that the nose is touched by the kiss of all foul and sweet air,
and the drums, and the throne of the faecal inlet,
and the eyes by its zig-zags.
So we drink Him and eat Him   60
and the watery Beaune and the stale cubes of Hovis
because He can jig
as near or as far from His Jigging Self
and as sad or lively as the chalice or the tray asks.
How's that, Antonio?

In the name of Bacon will you chicken me up that egg.
Shall I swallow cave-phantoms?

Anna Maria!
She reads Moses and says her love is crucified.
Leider! Leider! she bloomed and withered,   70
a pale abusive parakeet in a mainstreet window.

No I believe every word of it I assure you.
Fallor, ergo sum!
The coy old frôleur!
He tolle'd and legge'd
and he buttoned on his redemptorist waistcoat.
No matter, let it pass.
I'm a bold boy I know
so I'm not my son
(even if I were a concierge)   80
nor Joachim my father's
but the chip of a perfect block that's neither old nor new,
the lonely petal of a great high bright rose.

Are you ripe at last,
my slim pale double-breasted turd?
How rich she smells,
this abortion of a fledgling!
I will eat it with a fish fork.
White and yolk and feathers.
Then I will rise and move moving   90
toward Rahab of the snows,
the murdering matinal pope-confessed amazon,
Christina the ripper.
Oh Weulles spare the blood of a Frank
who has climbed the bitter steps,
(René du Perron . . .!)
and grant me my second
starless inscrutable hour.

Notes

René Descartes, Seigneur du Perron, liked his omelette made of eggs hatched from eight to ten days; shorter or longer under the hen and the result, he says, is disgusting.
He kept his own birthday to himself so that no astrologer could cast his nativity.
The shuttle of a ripening egg combs the warp of his days.

3 In 1640 the brothers Boot refuted Aristotle in Dublin.

4 Descartes passed on the easier problems in analytical geometry to his valet Gillot.

5–10 Refer to his contempt for Galileo Jr., (whom he confused with the more musical Galileo Sr.), and to his expedient sophistry concerning the movement of the earth.

17 He solved problems submitted by these mathematicians.

21–26 The attempt at swindling on the part of his elder brother Pierre de la Bretaillière – The money he received as a soldier.

27 Franz Hals.

29–30 As a child he played with a little cross-eyed girl.

31–35 His daughter died of scarlet fever at the age of six.

37–40 Honoured Harvey for his discovery of the circulation of the blood, but would not admit that he had explained the motion of the heart.

41 The heart of Henri IV was received at the Jesuit college of La Flèche while Descartes was still a student there.

45–53 His visions and pilgrimage to Loretto.

56–65 His Eucharistic sophistry, in reply to the Jansenist Antoine Arnauld, who challenged him to reconcile his doctrine of matter with the doctrine of transubstantiation.

68 Schurmann, the Dutch blue-stocking, a pious pupil of Voët, the adversary of Descartes.

8

Gnome

Spend the years of learning squandering
Courage for the years of wandering
Through a world politely turning
From the loutishness of learning.

Echo's Bones and Other Precipitates

The Vulture

dragging his hunger through the sky
of my skull shell of sky and earth

stooping to the prone who must
soon take up their life and walk

mocked by a tissue that may not serve
till hunger earth and sky be offal

Enueg I

Exeo in a spasm
tired of my darling's red sputum
from the Portobello Private Nursing Home
its secret things
and toil to the crest of the surge of the steep perilous bridge
and lapse down blankly under the scream of the hoarding
round the bright stiff banner of the hoarding
into a black west
throttled with clouds.

Above the mansions the algum-trees
the mountains
my skull sullenly
clot of anger
skewered aloft strangled in the cang of the wind
bites like a dog against its chastisement.

I trundle along rapidly now on my ruined feet
flush with the livid canal;
at Parnell Bridge a dying barge
carrying a cargo of nails and timber
rocks itself softly in the foaming cloister of the lock;
on the far bank a gang of down and outs would seem to
    be mending a beam.

Then for miles only wind
and the weals creeping alongside on the water
and the world opening up to the south
across a travesty of champaign to the mountains
and the stillborn evening turning a filthy green
manuring the night fungus
and the mind annulled
wrecked in wind.

I splashed past a little wearish old man,
Democritus,
scuttling along between a crutch and a stick,
his stump caught up horribly, like a claw, under his
    breech, smoking.
Then because a field on the left went up in a sudden blaze
of shouting and urgent whistling and scarlet and blue ganzies
I stopped and climbed the bank to see the game.
A child fidgeting at the gate called up:
'Would we be let in Mister?'
'Certainly' I said 'you would.'
But, afraid, he set off down the road.
'Well' I called after him 'why wouldn't you go on in?'
'Oh' he said, knowingly,
'I was in that field before and I got put out.'
So on,
derelict,
as from a bush of gorse on fire in the mountain after dark,
or in Sumatra the jungle hymen,
the still flagrant rafflesia.

Next:
a lamentable family of grey verminous hens,
perishing out in the sunk field,
trembling, half asleep, against the closed door of a shed,
with no means of roosting.
The great mushy toadstool,
green-black,
oozing up after me,
soaking up the tattered sky like an ink of pestilence,
in my skull the wind going fetid,
the water . . .

Next:
on the hill down from the Fox and Geese into Chapelizod
a small malevolent goat, exiled on the road,
remotely pucking the gate of his field;
the Isolde Stores a great perturbation of sweaty heroes,
in their Sunday best,
come hastening down for a pint of nepenthe or moly or
    half and half
from watching the hurlers above in Kilmainham.

Blotches of doomed yellow in the pit of the Liffey;
the fingers of the ladders hooked over the parapet,
soliciting;
a slush of vigilant gulls in the grey spew of the sewer.

Ah the banner
the banner of meat bleeding
on the silk of the seas and the arctic flowers
that do not exist.

Enueg II

world world world world
and the face grave
cloud against the evening

de morituris nihil nisi

and the face crumbling shyly
too late to darken the sky
blushing away into the evening
shuddering away like a gaffe

veronica mundi
veronica munda
gives us a wipe for the love of Jesus

sweating like Judas
tired of dying
tired of policemen
feet in marmalade
perspiring profusely
heart in marmalade
smoke more fruit
the old heart the old heart
breaking outside congress
doch I assure thee

lying on O'Connell Bridge

goggling at the tulips of the evening
the green tulips
shining round the corner like an anthrax
shining on Guinness's barges

the overtone the face
too late to brighten the sky
doch doch I assure thee

Alba

before morning you shall be here
and Dante and the Logos and all strata and mysteries
and the branded moon
beyond the white plane of music
that you shall establish here before morning

grave suave singing silk
stoop to the black firmament of areca
rain on the bamboos flower of smoke alley of willows

who though you stoop with fingers of compassion
to endorse the dust
shall not add to your bounty
whose beauty shall be a sheet before me
a statement of itself drawn across the tempest of emblems
so that there is no sun and no unveiling
and no host
only I and then the sheet
and bulk dead

Dortmunder

In the magic the Homer dusk
past the red spire of sanctuary
I null she royal hulk
hasten to the violet lamp to the thin K'in music of the bawd.
She stands before me in the bright stall
sustaining the jade splinters
the scarred signaculum of purity quiet
the eyes the eyes black till the plagal east
shall resolve the long night phrase.
Then, as a scroll, folded,
and the glory of her dissolution enlarged
in me, Habbakuk, mard of all sinners.
Schopenhauer is dead, the bawd
puts her lute away.

Sanies I

all the livelong way this day of sweet showers from
   Portrane on the seashore
Donabate sad swans of Turvey Swords
pounding along in three ratios like a sonata
like a Ritter with pommelled scrotum atra cura on the step
Botticelli from the fork down pestling the transmission
tires bleeding voiding zeep the highway
all heaven in the sphincter
the sphincter

müüüüüüüde now
potwalloping now through the promenaders
this trusty all-steel this super-real
bound for home like a good boy
where I was born with a pop with the green of the larches
ah to be back in the caul now with no trusts
no fingers no spoilt love
belting along in the meantime clutching the bike
the billows of the nubile the cere wrack
pot-valiant caulless waisted in rags hatless
for mamma papa chicken and ham
warm Grave too say the word
happy days snap the stem shed a tear
this day Spy Wedsday seven pentades past
oh the larches the pain drawn like a cork
the glans he took the day off up hill and down dale
with a ponderous fawn from the Liverpool London and
   Globe
back the shadows lengthen the sycomores are sobbing
to roly-poly oh to me a spanking boy

buckets of fizz childbed is thirsty work
for the midwife he is gory
for the proud parent he washes down a gob of gladness
for footsore Achates also he pants his pleasure
sparkling beestings for me
tired now hair ebbing gums ebbing ebbing home
good as gold now in the prime after a brief prodigality
yea and suave
suave urbane beyond good and evil
biding my time without rancour you may take your oath
distraught half-crooked courting the sneers of these fauns
    these smart nymphs
clipped like a pederast as to one trouser-end
sucking in my bloated lantern behind a Wild Woodbine
cinched to death in a filthy slicker
flinging the proud Swift forward breasting the swell of
    Stürmers
I see main verb at last
her whom alone in the accusative
I have dismounted to love
gliding towards me dauntless nautch-girl on the face of the
    waters
dauntless daughter of desires in the old black and flamingo
get along with you now take the six the seven the eight or
    the little single-decker
take a bus for all I care walk cadge a lift
home to the cob of your web in Holles Street
and let the tiger go on smiling
in our hearts that funds ways home

Sanies II

there was a happy land
the American Bar
in Rue Mouffetard
there were red eggs there
I have a dirty I say henorrhoids
coming from the bath
the steam the delight the sherbet
the chagrin of the old skinnymalinks
slouching happy body
loose in my stinking old suit
sailing slouching up to Puvis the gauntlet of tulips
lash lash me with yaller tulips I will let down
my stinking old trousers
my love she sewed up the pockets alive the live-oh she did
    she said that was better
spotless then within the brown rags gliding
frescoward free up the fjord of dyed eggs and thongbells
I disappear don't you know into the local
the mackerel are at billiards there they are crying the scores
the Barfrau makes a big impression with her mighty bottom
Dante and blissful Beatrice are there
prior to Vita Nuova
the balls splash no luck comrade
Gracieuse is there Belle-Belle down the drain
booted Percinet with his cobalt jowl
they are necking gobble-gobble
suck is not suck that alters

lo Alighieri has got off au revoir to all that
I break down quite in a titter of despite
hark
upon the saloon a terrible hush
a shiver convulses Madame de la Motte
it courses it peals down her collops
the great bottom foams into stillness
quick quick the cavaletto supplejacks for mumbo-jumbo
vivas puellas mortui incurrrrrsant boves
oh subito subito ere she recover the cang bamboo for
    bastinado
a bitter moon fessade à la mode
oh Becky spare me I have done thee no wrong spare me
    damn thee
spare me good Becky
call off thine adders Becky I will compensate thee in full
Lord have mercy upon
Christ have mercy upon us

Lord have mercy upon us

Serena I

without the grand old British Museum
Thales and the Aretino
on the bosom of the Regent's Park the phlox
crackles under the thunder
scarlet beauty in our world dead fish adrift
all things full of gods
pressed down and bleeding
a weaver-bird is tangerine the harpy is past caring
the condor likewise in his mangy boa
they stare out across monkey-hill the elephants
Ireland
the light creeps down their old home canyon
sucks me aloof to that old reliable
the burning btm of George the drill
ah across the way a adder
broaches her rat
white as snow
in her dazzling oven strom of peristalsis
limae labor

ah father father that art in heaven

I find me taking the Crystal Palace
for the Blessed Isles from Primrose Hill
alas I must be that kind of person
hence in Ken Wood who shall find me

my breath held in the midst of thickets
none but the most quarried lovers

I surprise me moved by the many a funnel hinged
for the obeisance to Tower Bridge
the viper's curtsy to and from the City
till in the dusk a lighter
blind with pride
tosses aside the scarf of the bascules
then in the grey hold of the ambulance
throbbing on the brink ebb of sighs
then I hug me below among the canaille
until a guttersnipe blast his cernèd eyes
demanding 'ave I done with the Mirror
I stump off in a fearful rage under Married Men's Quarters
Bloody Tower
and afar off at all speed screw me up Wren's giant bully
and curse the day caged panting on the platform
under the flaring urn
I was not born Defoe

but in Ken Wood
who shall find me

my brother the fly
the common housefly
sidling out of darkness into light
fastens on his place in the sun
whets his six legs
revels in his planes his poisers
it is the autumn of his life
he could not serve typhoid and mammon

Serena II

this clonic earth

see-saw she is blurred in sleep
she is fat half dead the rest is free-wheeling
part the black shag the pelt
is ashen woad
snarl and howl in the wood wake all the birds
hound the harlots out of the ferns
this damfool twilight threshing in the brake
bleating to be bloodied
this crapulent hush
tear its heart out

in her dreams she trembles again
way back in the dark old days panting
in the claws of the Pins in the stress of her hour
the bag writhes she thinks she is dying
the light fails it is time to lie down
Clew Bay vat of xanthic flowers
Croagh Patrick waned Hindu to spite a pilgrim
she is ready she has lain down above all the islands of glory
straining now this Sabbath evening of garlands
with a yo-heave-ho of able-bodied swans
out from the doomed land their reefs of tresses
in a hag she drops her young
the whales in Blacksod Bay are dancing

the asphodels come running the flags after
she thinks she is dying she is ashamed

she took me up on to a watershed
whence like the rubrics of a childhood
behold Meath shining through a chink in the hills
posses of larches there is no going back on
a rout of tracks and streams fleeing to the sea
kindergartens of steeples and then the harbour
like a woman making to cover her breasts
and left me

with whatever trust of panic we went out
with so much shall we return
there shall be no loss of panic between a man and his dog
bitch though he be

sodden packet of Churchman
muzzling the cairn
it is worse than dream
the light randy slut can't be easy
this clonic earth
all these phantoms shuddering out of focus
it is useless to close the eyes
all the chords of the earth broken like a woman pianist's
the toads abroad again on their rounds
sidling up to their snares
the fairy-tales of Meath ended
so say your prayers now and go to bed
your prayers before the lamps start to sing behind the larches
here at these knees of stone
then to bye-bye on the bones

Serena III

fix this pothook of beauty on this palette
you never know it might be final

or leave her she is paradise and then
plush hymens on your eyeballs

or on Butt Bridge blush for shame
the mixed declension of those mammae
cock up thy moon thine and thine only
up up up to the star of evening
swoon upon the arch-gasometer
on Misery Hill brand-new carnation
swoon upon the little purple
house of prayer
something heart of Mary
the Bull and Pool Beg that will never meet
not in this world

whereas dart away through the cavorting scapes
bucket o'er Victoria Bridge that's the idea
slow down slink down the Ringsend Road
Irishtown Sandymount puzzle find the Hell Fire
the Merrion Flats scored with a thrillion sigmas
Jesus Christ Son of God Saviour His Finger
girls taken strippin that's the idea
on the Bootersgrad breakwind and water
the tide making the dun gulls in a panic
the sands quicken in your hot heart
hide yourself not in the Rock keep on the move
keep on the move

Malacoda

thrice he came
the undertaker's man
impassible behind his scutal bowler
to measure
is he not paid to measure
this incorruptible in the vestibule
this malebranca knee-deep in the lilies
Malacoda knee-deep in the lilies
Malacoda for all the expert awe
that felts his perineum mutes his signal
sighing up through the heavy air
must it be it must be it must be
find the weeds engage them in the garden
hear she may see she need not

to coffin
with assistant ungulata
find the weeds engage their attention
hear she must see she need not

to cover
to be sure cover cover all over
your targe allow me hold your sulphur
divine dogday glass set fair
stay Scarmilion stay stay
lay this Huysum on the box
mind the imago it is he
hear she must see she must
all aboard all souls
half-mast aye aye

nay

Da Tagte Es

redeem the surrogate goodbyes
the sheet astream in your hand
who have no more for the land
and the glass unmisted above your eyes

Echo's Bones

asylum under my tread all this day
their muffled revels as the flesh falls
breaking without fear or favour wind
the gantelope of sense and nonsense run
taken by the maggots for what they are

★ ★ ★

Yoke of Liberty

The lips of her desire are grey
and parted like a silk loop
threatening
a slight wanton wound.
She preys wearily
on sensitive wild things
proud to be torn
by the grave crouch of her beauty.
But she will die and her snare
tendered so patiently
to my tamed watchful sorrow
will break and hang
in a pitiful crescent.

Antipepsis

And the number was uneven
In the green of holy Stephen
Where before the ass the cart
Was harnessed for a foreign part.
In this should not be seen the sign
Of hasard, no, but of design,
For of the two, by common consent,
The cart was the more intelligent.
Whose exceptionally pia
Mater hatched this grand idea
Is not known. He or she,
Smiling, unmolested, free,
By this one act the mind become
A providential vacuum,
Continues still to stroll amok,
To eat, drink, piss, shit, fart and fuck,
Assuming that the fucking season
Did not expire with that of reason.
Now through the city spreads apace
The cry: A thought has taken place!
A human thought! Ochone! Ochone!
Purissima Virgo! We're undone!
Bitched, buggered and bewilderèd!
Bring forth your dead! Bring forth your dead!

Cascando

why not merely the despaired of
occasion of
wordshed

is it not better abort than be barren

the hours after you are gone are so leaden
they will always start dragging too soon
the grapples clawing blindly the bed of want
bringing up the bones the old loves
sockets filled once with eyes like yours
all always is it better too soon than never
the black want splashing their faces
saying again nine days never floated the loved
nor nine months
nor nine lives

2
saying again
if you do not teach me I shall not learn
saying again there is a last
even of last times
last times of begging
last times of loving
of knowing not knowing pretending
a last even of last times of saying
if you do not love me I shall not be loved
if I do not love you I shall not love

the churn of stale words in the heart again
love love love thud of the old plunger
pestling the unalterable
whey of words

terrified again
of not loving
of loving and not you
of being loved and not by you
of knowing not knowing pretending
pretending

I and all the others that will love you
if they love you

3
unless they love you

Ooftish

offer it up plank it down
Golgotha was only the potegg
cancer angina it is all one to us
cough up your T.B. don't be stingy
no trifle is too trifling not even a thrombus
anything venereal is especially welcome
that old toga in the mothballs
don't be sentimental you won't be wanting it again
send it along we'll put it in the pot with the rest
with your love requited and unrequited
the things taken too late the things taken too soon
the spirit aching bullock's scrotum
you won't cure it you won't endure it
it is you it equals you any fool has to pity you
so parcel up the whole issue and send it along
the whole misery diagnosed undiagnosed misdiagnosed
get your friends to do the same we'll make use of it
we'll make sense of it we'll put it in the pot with the rest
it all boils down to blood of lamb

[Poems in French, 1937–1939]

elles viennent
autres et pareilles
avec chacune c'est autre et c'est pareil
avec chacune l'absence d'amour est autre
avec chacune l'absence d'amour est pareille

they come
different and the same
with each it is different and the same
with each the absence of love is different
with each the absence of love is the same

être là sans mâchoires sans dents
où s'en va le plaisir de perdre
avec celui à peine inférieur
de gagner
et Roscelin et on attend
adverbe oh petit cadeau
vide vide sinon des loques de chanson
mon père m'a donné un mari
ou en faisant la fleur
qu'elle mouille
tant qu'elle voudra jusqu'à l'élégie
des sabots ferrés encore loin des Halles
ou l'eau de la canaille pestant dans les tuyaux
ou plus rien
qu'elle mouille puisque c'est ainsi
parfasse tout le superflu
et vienne
à la bouche idiote à la main formicante
au bloc cave à l'œil qui écoute
de lointains coups de ciseaux argentins

Ascension

à travers la mince cloison
ce jour où un enfant
prodigue à sa façon
rentra dans sa famille
j'entends la voix
elle est émue elle commente
la coupe du monde de football

toujours trop jeune

en même temps par la fenêtre ouverte
par les airs tout court
sourdement
la houle des fidèles

son sang gicla avec abondance
sur les draps sur les pois de senteur sur son mec
de ses doigts dégoûtants il ferma les paupières
sur les grands yeux verts étonnés

elle rode légère
sur ma tombe d'air

La Mouche

entre la scène et moi
la vitre
vide sauf elle

ventre à terre
sanglée dans ses boyaux noirs
antennes affolées ailes liées
pattes crochues bouche suçant à vide
sabrant l'azur s'écrasant contre l'invisible
sous mon pouce impuissant elle fait chavirer
la mer et le ciel serein

ainsi a-t-on beau
par le beau temps et par le mauvais
enfermé chez soi enfermé chez eux
comme si c'était d'hier se rappeler le mammouth
le dinothérium les premiers baisers
les périodes glaciaires n'apportant rien de neuf
la grande chaleur du treizième de leur ère
sur Lisbonne fumante Kant froidement penché
rêver en générations de chênes et oublier son père
ses yeux s'il portait la moustache
s'il était bon de quoi il est mort
on n'en est pas moins mangé sans appétit
par le mauvais temps et par le pire
enfermé chez soi enfermé chez eux

Dieppe

encore le dernier reflux
le galet mort
le demi-tour puis les pas
vers les vieilles lumières

Dieppe

again the last ebb
the dead shingle
the turning then the steps
towards the lights of old

Rue de Vaugirard

à mi-hauteur
je débraye et béant de candeur
expose la plaque aux lumières et aux ombres
puis repars fortifié
d'un négatif irrécusable

Arènes de Lutèce

De là où nous sommes assis plus haut que les gradins
je nous vois entrer du côté de la Rue des Arènes,
hésiter, regarder en l'air, puis pesamment
venir vers nous à travers le sable sombre,
de plus en plus laids, aussi laids que les autres,
mais muets. Un petit chien vert
entre en courant du côté de la Rue Monge,
elle s'arrête, elle le suit des yeux,
il traverse l'arène, il disparait
derrière le socle du savant Gabriel de Mortillet.
Elle se retourne, je suis parti, je gravis seul
les marches rustiques, je touche de ma main gauche
la rampe rustique, elle est en béton. Elle hésite,
fait un pas vers la sortie de la Rue Monge, puis me suit.
J'ai un frisson, c'est moi qui me rejoins,
c'est avec d'autres yeux que maintenant je regarde
le sable, les flaques d'eau sous la bruine,
une petite fille traînant derrière elle un cerceau,
un couple, qui sait des amoureux, la main dans la main,
les gradins vides, les hautes maisons, le ciel
qui nous éclaire trop tard.
Je me retourne, je suis étonné
de trouver là son triste visage.

Saint-Lô

Vire will wind in other shadows
unborn through the bright ways tremble
and the old mind ghost-forsaken
sink into its havoc

[Poems in French, 1947–1949]

bon bon il est un pays
où l'oubli où pèse l'oubli
doucement sur les mondes innommés
là la tête on la tait la tête est muette
et on sait non on ne sait rien
le chant des bouches mortes meurt
sur la grève il a fait le voyage
il n'y a rien à pleurer

ma solitude je la connais allez je la connais mal
j'ai le temps c'est ce que je me dis j'ai le temps
mais quel temps os affamé le temps du chien
du ciel pâlissant sans cesse mon grain de ciel
du rayon qui grimpe ocellé tremblant
des microns des années ténèbres

vous voulez que j'aille d'A à B je ne peux pas
je ne peux pas sortir je suis dans un pays sans traces
oui oui c'est une belle chose que vous avez là une bien
    belle chose
qu'est-ce que c'est ne me posez plus de questions
spirale poussière d'instants qu'est-ce que c'est le même
le calme l'amour la haine le calme le calme

Mort de A.D.

et là être là encore là
pressé contre ma vieille planche vérolée du noir
des jours et nuits broyés aveuglément
à être là à ne pas fuir et fuir et être là
courbé vers l'aveu du temps mourant
d'avoir été ce qu'il fut fait ce qu'il fit
de moi de mon ami mort hier l'œil luisant
les dents longues haletant dans sa barbe dévorant
la vie des saints une vie par jour de vie
revivant dans la nuit ses noirs péchés
mort hier pendant que je vivais
et être là buvant plus haut que l'orage
la coulpe du temps irrémissible
agrippé au vieux bois témoin des départs
témoin des retours

vive morte ma seule saison
lis blancs chrysanthèmes
nids vifs abandonnés
boue des feuilles d'avril
beaux jours gris de givre

je suis ce cours de sable qui glisse
entre le galet et la dune
la pluie d'été pleut sur ma vie
sur moi ma vie qui me fuit me poursuit
et finira le jour de son commencement

cher instant je te vois
dans ce rideau de brume qui recule
où je n'aurai plus à fouler ces longs seuils mouvants
et vivrai le temps d'une porte
qui s'ouvre et se referme

my way is in the sand flowing
between the shingle and the dune
the summer rain rains on my life
on me my life harrying fleeing
to its beginning to its end

my peace is there in the receding mist
when I may cease from treading these long shifting
    thresholds
and live the space of a door
that opens and shuts

que ferais-je sans ce monde sans visage sans questions
où être ne dure qu'un instant où chaque instant
verse dans le vide dans l'oubli d'avoir été
sans cette onde où à la fin
corps et ombre ensemble s'engloutissent
que ferais-je sans ce silence gouffre des murmures
haletant furieux vers le secours vers l'amour
sans ce ciel qui s'élève
sur la poussière de ses lests

que ferais-je je ferais comme hier comme aujourd'hui
regardant par mon hublot si je ne suis pas seul
à errer et à virer loin de toute vie
dans un espace pantin
sans voix parmi les voix
enfermées avec moi

what would I do without this world faceless incurious
where to be lasts but an instant where every instant
spills in the void the ignorance of having been
without this wave where in the end
body and shadow together are engulfed
what would I do without this silence where the murmurs die
the pantings the frenzies towards succour towards love
without this sky that soars
above its ballast dust

what would I do what I did yesterday and the day before
peering out of my deadlight looking for another
wandering like me eddying far from all the living
in a convulsive space
among the voices voiceless
that throng my hiddenness

je voudrais que mon amour meure
qu'il pleuve sur le cimetière
et les ruelles où je vais
pleurant celle qui crut m'aimer

I would like my love to die
and the rain to be raining on the graveyard
and on me walking the streets
mourning her who thought she loved me

Song

Age is when to a man
Huddled o'er the ingle
Shivering for the hag
To put the pan in the bed
And bring the toddy
She comes in the ashes
Who loved could not be won
Or won not loved
Or some other trouble
Comes in the ashes
Like in that old light
The face in the ashes
That old starlight
On the earth again.

hors crâne seul dedans
quelque part quelquefois
comme quelque chose

crâne abri dernier
pris dans le dehors
tel Bocca dans la glace

l'œil à l'alarme infime
s'ouvre bée se rescelle
n'y ayant plus rien

ainsi quelquefois
comme quelque chose
de la vie pas forcément

Something there

something there
where
out there
out where
outside
what
the head what else
something there somewhere outside
the head

at the faint sound so brief
it is gone and the whole globe
not yet bare
the eye
opens wide
wide
till in the end
nothing more
shutters it again

so the odd time
out there
somewhere out there
like as if
as if
something
not life
necessarily

dread nay

head fast
in out as dead
till rending
long still
faint stir
unseal the eye
till still again
seal again

head sphere
ashen smooth
one eye
no hint when to
then glare
cyclop no
one side
eerily

on face
of out spread
vast in
the highmost
snow white
sheeting all
asylum head
sole blot

faster than where
in hellice eyes
stream till
frozen to
jaws rail

gnaw gnash
teeth with stork
clack chatter

come through
no sense and gone
while eye
shocked wide
with white
still to bare
stir dread
nay to nought

sudden in
ashen smooth
aghast
glittering rent
till sudden
smooth again
stir so past
never been

at ray
in latibule
long dark
stir of dread
till breach
long sealed
dark again
still again

so ere
long still
long nought
rent so
so stir
long past
head fast
in out as dead

Roundelay

on all that strand
at end of day
steps sole sound
long sole sound
until unbidden stay
then no sound
on all that strand
long no sound
until unbidden go
steps sole sound
long sole sound
on all that strand
at end of day

mirlitonnades

en face
le pire
jusqu'à ce
qu'il fasse rire

rentrer
à la nuit
au logis
allumer

éteindre voir
la nuit voir
collé à la vitre
le visage

somme toute
tout compte fait
un quart de milliasse
de quarts d'heure
sans compter
les temps morts

fin fond du néant
au bout de quelle guette
l'œil crut entrevoir
remuer faiblement
la tête le calma disant
ce ne fut que dans ta tête

silence tel que ce qui fut
avant jamais ne sera plus
par le murmure déchiré
d'une parole sans passé
d'avoir trop dit n'en pouvant plus
jurant de ne se taire plus

écoute-les
s'ajouter
les mots
aux mots
sans mot
les pas
aux pas
un à
un

lueurs lisières
de la navette
plus qu'un pas s'éteignent
demi-tour remiroitent

halte plutôt
loin des deux
chez soi sans soi
ni eux

imagine si ceci
un jour ceci
un beau jour
imagine
si un jour
un beau jour ceci
cessait
imagine

d'abord
à plat sur du dur
la droite
ou la gauche
n'importe

ensuite
à plat sur la droite
ou la gauche
la gauche
ou la droite

enfin
à plat sur la gauche
ou la droite
n'importe
sur le tout
la tête

flux cause
que toute chose
tout en étant
toute chose
donc celle-là
même celle-là
tout en étant
n'est pas
parlons-en

samedi répit
plus rire
depuis minuit
jusqu'à minuit
pas pleurer

chaque jour envie
d'être un jour en vie
non certes sans regret
un jour d'être né

nuit qui fais tant
implorer l'aube
nuit de grâce
tombe

rien nul
n'aura été
pour rien
tant été
rien
nul

à peine à bien mené
le dernier pas le pied
repose en attendant
comme le veut l'usage
que l'autre en fasse autant
comme le veut l'usage
et porte ainsi le faix
encore de l'avant
comme le veut l'usage
enfin jusqu'à présent

ce qu'ont les yeux
mal vu de bien
les doigts laissé
de bien filer
serre-les bien
les doigts les yeux
le bien revient
en mieux

ce qu'a de pis
le cœur connu
la tête pu
de pis se dire
fais-les
ressusciter
le pis revient
en pire

ne manquez pas à Tanger
le cimetière Saint-André
morts sous un fouillis
de fleurs surensevelis
banc à la mémoire
d'Arthur Keyser
de cœur avec lui
restes dessus assis

plus loin un autre commémore
Caroline Hay Taylor
fidèle à sa philosophie
qu'espoir il y a tant qu'il y a vie
d'Irlande elle s'enfuit aux cieux
en août mil neuf cent trente-deux

ne manquez pas à Stuttgart
la longue Rue Neckar
du néant là l'attrait
n'est plus ce qu'il était
tant le soupçon est fort
d'y être déjà et d'ores

vieil aller
vieux arrêts

aller
absent
absent
arrêter

fous qui disiez
plus jamais
vite
redites

pas à pas
nulle part
nul seul
ne sait comment
petits pas
nulle part
obstinément

rêve
sans fin
ni trêve
à rien

morte parmi
ses mouches mortes
un souffle coulis
berce l'araignée

d'où
la voix qui dit
vis

d'une autre vie

mots survivants
de la vie
encore un moment
tenez-lui compagnie

fleuves et océans
l'ont laissé pour vivant
au ru de Courtablon
près la Mare-Chaudron

de pied ferme
tout en n'attendant plus
il se passe devant
allant sans but

sitôt sorti de l'ermitage
ce fut le calme après l'orage

à l'instant de s'entendre dire
ne plus en avoir pour longtemps
la vie à lui enfin sourire
se mit de toutes ses dents

la nuit venue où l'âme allait
enfin lui être réclamée
voilà-t-il pas qu'incontinent
il la rendit une heure avant

pas davantage
de souvenirs qu'à l'âge
d'avril un jour
d'un jour

son ombre une nuit
lui reparut
s'allongea pâlit
se dissolut

noire sœur
qui es aux enfers
à tort tranchant
et à travers
qu'est-ce que tu attends

le nain nonagénaire
dans un dernier murmure
de grâce au moins la bière
grandeur nature

à bout de songes un bouquin
au gîte à dire adieu astreint
de chasse lasse fit exprès
d'oublier le chandelier

one dead of night
in the dead still
he looked up
from his book

from that dark
to pore on other dark

till afar
taper faint
the eyes

in the dead still

till afar
his book as by
a hand not his
a hand on his
faintly closed

for good or ill

for good and ill

there
the life late led
down there
all done unsaid

again gone
with what to tell
on again
retell

bail bail till better
founder

Là

aller là où jamais avant
à peine là que là toujours
où que là où jamais avant
à peine là que là toujours

go where never before
no sooner there than there always
no matter where never before
no sooner there than there always

Brief Dream

Go end there
One fine day
Where never till then
Till as much as to say
No matter where
No matter when

Comment dire

folie –
folie que de –
que de –
comment dire –
folie que de ce –
depuis –
folie depuis ce –
donné –
folie donné ce que de –
vu –
folie vu ce –
ce –
comment dire –
ceci –
ce ceci –
ceci-ci –
tout ce ceci-ci –
folie donné tout ce –
vu –
folie vu tout ce ceci-ci que de –
que de –
comment dire –
voir –
entrevoir –
croire entrevoir –
vouloir croire entrevoir –
folie que de vouloir croire entrevoir quoi –
quoi –
comment dire –
et où –

what is the word

folly –
folly for to –
for to –
what is the word –
folly from this –
all this –
folly from all this –
given –
folly given all this –
seeing –
folly seeing all this –
this –
what is the word –
this this –
this this here –
all this this here –
folly given all this –
seeing –
folly seeing all this this here –
for to –
what is the word –
see –
glimpse –
seem to glimpse –
need to seem to glimpse –
folly for to need to seem to glimpse –
what –
what is the word –
and where –

que de vouloir croire entrevoir quoi où –
où –
comment dire –
là –
là-bas –
loin –
loin là là-bas –
à peine –
loin là là-bas à peine quoi –
quoi –
comment dire –
vu tout ceci –
tout ce ceci-ci –
folie que de voir quoi –
entrevoir –
croire entrevoir –
vouloir croire entrevoir –
loin là là-bas à peine quoi –
folie que d'y vouloir croire entrevoir quoi –
quoi –
comment dire –

comment dire

folly for to need to seem to glimpse what where –
where –
what is the word –
there –
over there –
away over there –
afar –
afar away over there –
afaint –
afaint afar away over there what –
what –
what is the word –
seeing all this –
all this this –
all this this here –
folly for to see what –
glimpse –
seem to glimpse –
need to seem to glimpse –
afaint afar away over there what –
folly for to need to seem to glimpse afaint afar away over there
    what –
what –
what is the word –

what is the word

[Translations by Samuel Beckett
of poems by others]

EUGENIO MONTALE

Delta

La vita che si rompe nei travasi
secreti a te ho legata:
quella che si dibatte in sé e par quasi
non ti sappia, presenza soffocata.

Quando il tempo s'ingorga alle sue dighe
la tua vicenda accordi alla sua immensa,
ed affiori, memoria, più palese
dall'oscura regione ove scendevi,
come ora, al dopopioggia, si riaddensa
il verde ai rami, ai muri il cinabrese.

Tutto ignoro di te fuor del messaggio
muto che mi sostenta sulla via:
se forma esisti o ubbia nella fumea
d'un sogno t'alimenta
la riviera che infebbra, torba, e scroscia
incontro alla marea.

Nulla di te nel vacillar dell'ore
bige o squarciate da un vampo di solfo
fuori che il fischio del rimorchiatore
che dalle brume approda al golfo.

Delta

To thee
I have willed the life drained
in secret transfusions, the life chained
in a coil of restlessness, unaware, self-angry.

When time leans on his dykes
then thine
be his allconsciousness
and memory flower forth in a flame
from the dark sanctuary, and shine
more brightly, as now, the rain over, the dragon's-blood
on the walls and the green against the branches.

Of thee
I know nothing, only
the tidings sustaining my going,
and shall I find
thee shape or the fumes of a dream
drawing life
from the river's fever boiling darkly
    against the tide.

Of thee nothing in the grey hours and the hours
torn by a flame of sulphur,
only
the whistle of the tug
whose prow has ridden forth into the bright gulf.

ERNST MOERMAN

Armstrong

Un jour qu'Armstrong jouait au loto avec ses sœurs
Il s'écria: 'C'est moi qui ai la viande crue'.
Il s'en fit des lèvres et depuis ce jour,
Sa trompette a la nostalgie de leur premier baiser.

Terre noire où fleurit le pavot,
Armstrong conduit le torrent, en robe d'épousée, au sommeil.

Chaque fois que, pour moi, 'Some of these days'
Traverse vingt épaisseurs de silence,
Il me vient un cheveu blanc
Dans un vertige d'ascenseur.

'After you're gone'
Est un miroir où la douleur se regarde vieillir.

'You driving me crazy' est une aube tremblante
Où sa trompette à la pupille dilatée
Se promène sans balancier sur les cordes de violon.

Et 'Confessing' donne de l'appétit au malheur.

Louis Armstrong

suddenly in the midst of a game of lotto with his sisters
Armstrong let a roar out of him that he had the raw meat
red wet flesh for Louis
and he up and he sliced him two rumplips
since when his trumpet bubbles
their fust buss

poppies burn on the black earth
he weds the flood he lulls her

some of these days muffled in ooze
down down down down
pang of white in my hair

after you're gone
Narcissus lean and slippered

you're driving me crazy and the trumpet
is Ole Bull it chassés aghast
out of the throes of morning
down the giddy catgut
and *confessing* and my woe slavers
the black music it can't be easy
it threshes the old heart into a spin
into a blaze

Chant de l'impatience, ta musique noctambule
Se répand dans mes veines où tout prend feu.
Armstrong, petit père Mississippi,
Le lac s'emplit de ta voix
Et la pluie remonte vers le ciel

Vers quels villages abordent tes flèches
Après nous avoir touchés?
Traversent-elles des chevaux sauvages
Avant de nous empoisonner?
Les racines de ton chant se mélangent dans la terre
En suivant les sillons que las foudre a tracés.
Les nuits de Harlem portent l'empreinte de tes ongles
Et la neige fond noire, au soleil de ton cœur.

Je marche, les yeux clos, vers un abîme
Où m'appellent les œillades de tes notes femelles
Plus inquiétantes que l'appel de la mer.

Louis lil' ole fader Mississippi
his voice gushes into the lake
the rain spouts back into heaven
his arrows from afar they fizz through the wild horses
they fang you and me
then they fly home

flurry of lightning in the earth
sockets for his rootbound song
nights of Harlem scored with his nails
snow black slush when his heart rises

his she-notes they have more tentacles than the sea
they woo me they close my eyes
they suck me out of the world

ARTHUR RIMBAUD

Le Bateau ivre

Comme je descendais des Fleuves impassibles,
Je ne me sentis plus guidé par les haleurs:
Des Peaux-Rouges criards les avaient pris pour cibles,
Les ayant cloués nus aux poteaux de couleurs.

J'étais insoucieux de tous les équipages,
Porteur de blés flamands ou de cotons anglais.
Quand avec mes haleurs ont fini ces tapages,
Les fleuves m'ont laissé descendre où je voulais.

Drunken Boat

Downstream on impassive rivers suddenly
I felt the towline of the boatmen slacken.
Redskins had taken them in a scream and stripped them and
Skewered them to the glaring stakes for targets.

Then, delivered from my straining boatmen,
From the trivial racket of trivial crews and from
The freights of Flemish grain and English cotton,
I made my own course down the passive rivers.

Dans les clapotements furieux des marées,
Moi, l'autre hiver, plus sourd que les cerveaux d'enfants,
Je courus! et les Péninsules démarrées
N'ont pas subi tohu-bohus plus triomphants.

La tempête a béni mes éveils maritimes.
Plus léger qu'un bouchon j'ai dansé sur les flots
Qu'on appelle rouleurs éternels de victimes,
Dix nuits, sans regretter l'œil niais des falots!

Plus douce qu'aux enfants la chair des pommes sures,
L'eau verte pénétra ma coque de sapin
Et des taches de vins bleus et des vomissures
Me lava, dispersant gouvernail et grappin.

Et dès lors, je me suis baigné dans le Poème
De la Mer, infusé d'astres, et lactescent,
Dévorant les azurs verts; où, flottaison blême
Et ravie, un noyé pensif, parfois descend;

Blanker than the brain of a child I fled
Through winter, I scoured the furious jolts of the tides,
In an uproar and a chaos of Peninsulas,
Exultant, from their moorings in triumph torn.

I started awake to tempestuous hallowings.
Nine nights I danced like a cork on the billows, I danced
On the breakers, sacrificial, for ever and ever,
And the crass eye of the lanterns was expunged.

More firmly bland than to children apples' firm pulp,
Soaked the green water through my hull of pine,
Scattering helm and grappling and washing me
Of the stains, the vomitings and blue wine.

Thenceforward, fused in the poem, milk of stars,
Of the sea, I coiled through deeps of cloudless green,
Where, dimly, they come swaying down,
Rapt and sad, singly, the drowned;

Où, teignant tout à coup les bleuités, délires
Et rhythmes lents sous les rutilements du jour,
Plus fortes que l'alcool, plus vastes que vos lyres,
Fermentent les rousseurs amères de l'amour!

Je sais les cieux crevant en éclairs, et les trombes
Et les ressacs et les courants: je sais le soir,
L'Aube exaltée ainsi qu'un peuple de colombes,
Et j'ai vu quelquefois ce que l'homme a cru voir!

J'ai vu le soleil bas, taché d'horreurs mystiques
Illuminant de longs figements violets,
Pareils à des acteurs de drames très antiques
Les flots roulant au loin leurs frissons de volets!

J'ai rêvé la nuit verte aux neiges éblouies,
Baiser montant aux yeux des mers avec lenteur,
La circulation des sèves inouïes,
Et l'éveil jaune et bleu des phosphores chanteurs!

Where, under the sky's haemorrhage, slowly tossing
In thuds of fever, arch-alcohol of song,
Pumping over the blues in sudden stains,
The bitter rednesses of love ferment.

I know the heavens split with lightnings and the currents
Of the sea and its surgings and its spoutings; I know evening,
And dawn exalted like a cloud of doves.
And my eyes have fixed phantasmagoria.

I have seen, as shed by ancient tragic footlights,
Out from the horror of the low sun's mystic stains,
Long weals of violet creep across the sea
And peals of ague rattle down its slats.

I have dreamt the green night's drifts of dazzled snow,
The slow climb of kisses to the eyes of the seas,
The circulation of unheard saps,
And the yellow-blue alarum of phosphors singing.

J'ai suivi, des mois pleins, pareille aux vacheries
Hystériques, la houle à l'assaut des récifs,
Sans songer que les pieds lumineux des Maries
Pussent forcer le muffle aux Océans poussifs!

J'ai heurté, savez-vous, d'incroyables Florides
Mêlant aux fleurs des yeux de panthères à peaux
D'hommes, des arcs-en-ciel tendus comme des brides
Sous l'horizon des mers, à de glauques troupeaux!

J'ai vu fermenter les marais, énormes nasses
Où pourrit dans les joncs tout un Léviathan,
Des écroulements d'eaux au milieu des bonaces
Et les lointains vers les gouffres cataractant!

Glaciers, soleils d'argent, flots nacreux, cieux de braises,
Échouages hideux au fond des golfes bruns
Où les serpents géants dévorés des punaises
Choient, des arbres tordus, avec de noirs parfums!

I have followed months long the maddened herds of the surf
Storming the reefs, mindless of the feet,
The radiant feet of the Marys that constrain
The stampedes of the broken-winded Oceans.

I have fouled, be it known, unspeakable Floridas, tangle of
The flowers of the eyes of panthers in the skins of
Men and the taut rainbows curbing,
Beyond the brows of the seas, the glaucous herds.

I have seen Leviathan sprawl rotting in the reeds
Of the great seething swamp-nets;
The calm sea disembowelled in waterslides
And the cataracting of the doomed horizons.

Iridescent waters, glaciers, suns of silver, flagrant skies,
And dark creeks' secret ledges, horror-strewn,
Where giant reptiles, pullulant with lice,
Lapse with dark perfumes from the writhing trees.

133

J'aurais voulu montrer aux enfants ces dorades
Du flot bleu, ces poissons d'or, ces poissons chantants.
Des écumes de fleurs ont béni mes dérades,
Et d'ineffables vents m'ont ailé par instants.

Parfois, martyr lassé des pôles et des zones,
La mer, dont le sanglot faisait mon roulis doux,
Montait vers moi ses fleurs d'ombre aux ventouses jaunes
Et je restais, ainsi qu'une femme à genoux . . .

Presque'île, ballottant sur mes bords les querelles
Et les fientes d'oiseaux clabaudeurs aux yeux blonds.
Et je voguais, lorsqu'à travers mes liens frêles
Des noyés descendaient dormir, à reculons!

Or moi, bateau perdu sous les cheveux des anses,
Jeté par l'ouragan dans l'éther sans oiseau,
Moi dont les Monitors et les voiliers des Hanses
N'auraient pas repêché la carcasse ivre d'eau;

I would have shown to children those dorados
Of the blue wave, those golden fish, those singing fish;
In spumes of flowers I have risen from my anchors
And canticles of wind have blessed my wings.

Then toward me, rocking softly on its sobbing,
Weary of the torment of the poles and zones,
The sea would lift its yellow polyps on flowers
Of gloom and hold me – like a woman kneeling –

A stranded sanctuary for screeching birds,
Flaxen-eyed, shiteing on my trembling decks,
Till down they swayed to sleep, the drowned, spreadeagled,
And, sundering the fine tendrils, floated me.

Now I who was wrecked in the inlets' tangled hair
And flung beyond birds aloft by the hurricane,
Whose carcass drunk with water Monitors
And Hanseatic sloops could not have salved;

Libre, fumant, monté de brumes violettes,
Moi qui trouais le ciel rougeoyant comme un mur
Qui porte, confiture exquise aux bons poètes,
Des lichens de soleil et des morves d'azur;

Qui courais, taché de lunules électriques,
Planche folle, escorté des hippocampes noirs,
Quand les juillets faisaient crouler à coups de triques
Les cieux ultramarins aux ardents entonnoirs;

Moi qui tremblais, sentant geindre à cinquante lieues
Le rut des Béhémots et des Maelstroms épais,
Fileur éternel des immobilités bleues,
Je regrette l'Europe aux anciens parapets!

J'ai vu des archipels sidéraux! et des îles
Dont les cieux délirants sont ouverts au vogueur:
– Est-ce en ces nuits sans fond que tu dors et t'exiles,
Million d'oiseaux d'or, ô future Vigueur? –

Who, reeking and free in a fume of purple spray,
Have pierced the skies that flame as a wall would flame
For a chosen poet's rapture, and stream and flame
With solar lichen and with azure snot;

Who scudded, with my escort of black sea-horses,
Fury of timber, scarred with electric moons,
When Sirius flogged into a drift of ashes
The furnace-cratered cobalt of the skies;

I who heard in trembling across a waste of leagues
The turgent Stroms and Behemoths moan their rut,
I weaving for ever voids of spellbound blue,
Now remember Europe and her ancient ramparts.

I saw archipelagoes of stars and islands launched me
Aloft on the deep delirium of their skies:
Are these the fathomless nights of your sleep and exile,
Million of golden birds, oh Vigour to be?

Mais, vrai, j'ai trop pleuré! Les Aubes sont navrantes.
Toute lune est atroce et tout soleil amer:
L'âcre amour m'a gonflé de torpeurs enivrantes.
O que ma quille éclate! O que j'aille à la mer!

Si je désire une eau d'Europe, c'est la flache
Noire et froide où vers le crépuscule embaumé
Un enfant accroupi, plein de tristesse, lâche
Un bateau frêle comme un papillon de mai.

Je ne puis plus, baigné de vos langueurs, ô lames,
Enlever leur sillage aux porteurs de cotons,
Ni traverser l'orgueil des drapeaux et des flammes,
Ni nager sous les yeux horribles des pontons.

But no more tears. Dawns have broken my heart,
And every moon is torment, every sun bitterness;
I am bloated with the stagnant fumes of acrid loving –
May I split from stem to stern and founder, ah founder!

I want none of Europe's waters unless it be
The cold black puddle where a child, full of sadness,
Squatting, looses a boat as frail
As a moth into the fragrant evening.

Steeped in the languors of the swell, I may
Absorb no more the wake of the cotton-freighters,
Nor breast the arrogant oriflammes and banners,
Nor swim beneath the leer of the pontoons.

PAUL ÉLUARD

L'amoureuse

Elle est debout sur mes paupières
Et ses cheveux sont dans les miens,
Elle a la forme de mes mains,
Elle a la couleur de mes yeux,
Elle s'engloutit dans mon ombre
Comme une pierre sur le ciel.

Elle a toujours les yeux ouverts
Et ne me laisse pas dormir.
Ses rêves en pleine lumière
Font s'évaporer les soleils,
Me font rire, pleurer et rire,
Parler sans avoir rien à dire.

Lady Love

She is standing on my lids
And her hair is in my hair,
She has the colour of my eye,
She has the body of my hand,
In my shade she is engulfed
As a stone against the sky.

She will never close her eyes
And she does not let me sleep.
And her dreams in the bright day
Make the suns evaporate,
And me laugh cry and laugh,
Speak when I have nothing to say.

A perte de vue dans le sens de mon corps

Tous les arbres toutes leurs branches toutes leurs feuilles
L'herbe à la base les rochers et les maisons en masse
Au loin la mer que ton œil baigne
Ces images d'un jour après l'autre
Les vices les vertus tellement imparfaits
La transparence des passants dans les rues de hasard
Et les passantes exhalées par tes recherches obstinées
Tes idées fixes au cœur de plomb aux lèvres vierges
Les vices les vertus tellement imparfaits
La ressemblance des regards de permission avec les yeux
    que tu conquis
La confusion des corps des lassitudes des ardeurs
L'imitation des mots des attitudes des idées
Les vices les vertus tellement imparfaits

L'amour c'est l'homme inachevé.

Out of Sight in the Direction of My Body

All the trees all their boughs all their leaves
The grass at the base the rocks the massed houses
Afar the sea that thine eye washes
Those images of one day and the next
The vices the virtues that are so imperfect
The transparence of men that pass in the streets of hazard
And women that pass in a fume from thy dour questing
The fixed ideas virgin-lipped leaden-hearted
The vices the virtues that are so imperfect
The eyes consenting resembling the eyes thou didst
    vanquish
The confusion of the bodies the lassitudes the ardours
The imitation of the words the attitudes the ideas
The vices the virtues that are so imperfect

Love is man unfinished.

GUILLAUME APOLLINAIRE

Zone

A la fin tu es las de ce monde ancien

Bergère ô tour Eiffel le troupeau des ponts bêle ce matin

Tu en as assez de vivre dans l'antiquité grecque et romaine

Ici même les automobiles ont l'air d'être anciennes
La religion seule est restée toute neuve la religion
Est restée simple comme les hangars de Port-Aviation

Seul en Europe tu n'es pas antique ô Christianisme
L'Européen le plus moderne c'est vous Pape Pie X
Et toi que les fenêtres observent la honte te retient
D'entrer dans une église et de t'y confesser ce matin
Tu lis les prospectus les catalogues les affiches qui
    chantent tout haut
Voilà la poésie ce matin et pour la prose il y a les journaux
Il y a les livraisons à 25 centimes pleines d'aventures
    policières
Portraits des grands hommes et mille titres divers

Zone

In the end you are weary of this ancient world

This morning the bridges are bleating Eiffel Tower oh herd

Weary of living in Roman antiquity and Greek

Here even the motor-cars look antique
Religion alone has stayed young religion
Has stayed simple like the hangars at Port Aviation

You alone in Europe Christianity are not ancient
The most modern European is you Pope Pius X
And you whom the windows watch shame restrains
From entering a church this morning and confessing your
    sins
You read the handbills the catalogues the singing posters
So much for poetry this morning and the prose is in
    the papers
Special editions full of crimes
Celebrities and other attractions for 25 centimes

J'ai vu ce matin une jolie rue dont j'ai oublié le nom
Neuve et propre du soleil elle était le clairon
Les directeurs les ouvriers et les belles sténo-dactylographes
Du lundi matin au samedi soir quatre fois par jour y passent
Le matin par trois fois la sirène y gémit
Une cloche rageuse y aboie vers midi
Les inscriptions des enseignes et des murailles
Les plaques les avis à la façon des perroquets criaillent
J'aime la grâce de cette rue industrielle
Située à Paris entre la rue Aumont-Thiéville et l'avenue
    des Ternes

Voilà la jeune rue et tu n'es encore qu'un petit enfant
Ta mère ne t'habille que de bleu et de blanc
Tu es très pieux et avec le plus ancien de tes camarades
    René Dalize
Vous n'aimez rien tant que les pompes de l'Église
Il est neuf heures le gaz est baissé tout bleu vous sortez
    du dortoir en cachette
Vous priez toute la nuit dans la chapelle du collège
Tandis qu'éternelle et adorable profondeur améthyste
Tourne à jamais la flamboyante gloire du Christ
C'est le beau lys que tous nous cultivons
C'est la torche aux cheveux roux que n'éteint pas le vent
C'est le fils pâle et vermeil de la douloureuse mère
C'est l'arbre toujours touffu de toutes les prières
C'est la double potence de l'honneur et de l'éternité
C'est l'étoile à six branches
C'est Dieu qui meurt le vendredi et ressuscite le dimanche

This morning I saw a pretty street whose name is gone
Clean and shining clarion of the sun
Where from Monday morning to Saturday evening four
    times a day
Directors workers and beautiful shorthand typists go their
    way
And thrice in the morning the siren makes its moan
And a bell bays savagely coming up to noon
The inscriptions on walls and signs
The notices and plates squawk parrot-wise
I love the grace of this industrial street
In Paris between the Avenue des Ternes and the Rue
    Aumont-Thiéville

There it is the young street and you still but a small child
Your mother always dresses you in blue and white
You are very pious and with René Dalize your oldest crony
Nothing delights you more than church ceremony
It is nine at night the lowered gas burns blue you steal away
From the dormitory and all night in the college chapel pray
Whilst everlastingly the flaming glory of Christ
Wheels in adorable depths of amethyst
It is the fair lily that we all revere
It is the torch burning in the wind its auburn hair
It is the rosepale son of the mother of grief
It is the tree with the world's prayers ever in leaf
It is of honour and eternity the double beam
It is the six-branched star it is God
Who Friday dies and Sunday rises from the dead

C'est le Christ qui monte au ciel mieux que les aviateurs
Il détient le record du monde pour la hauteur

Pupille Christ de l'œil
Vingtième pupille des siècles il sait y faire
Et changé en oiseau ce siècle comme Jésus monte dans l'air
Les diables dans les abîmes lèvent la tête pour le regarder
Ils disent qu'il imite Simon Mage en Judée
Ils crient s'il sait voler qu'on l'appelle voleur
Les anges voltigent autour du joli voltigeur
Icare Enoch Élie Apollonius de Thyane
Flottent autour du premier aéroplane
Ils s'écartent parfois pour laisser passer ceux que transporte
    la Sainte-Eucharistie
Ces prêtres qui montent éternellement élevant l'hostie
L'avion se pose enfin sans refermer les ailes
Le ciel s'emplit alors de millions d'hirondelles
A tire-d'aile viennent les corbeaux les faucons les hiboux
D'Afrique arrivent les ibis les flamants les marabouts
L'oiseau Roc célébré par les conteurs et les poètes
Plane tenant dans ses serres le crâne d'Adam la première tête
L'aigle fond de l'horizon en poussant un grand cri
Et d'Amérique vient le petit colibri
De Chine sont venus ses pihis longs et souples
Qui n'ont qu'une seule aile et qui volent par couples
Puis voici la colombe esprit immaculé
Qu'escortent l'oiseau-lyre et le paon ocellé
Le phénix ce bûcher qui soi-même s'engendre

It is Christ who better than airmen wings his flight
Holding the record of the world for height

Pupil Christ of the eye
Twentieth pupil of the centuries it is no novice
And changed into a bird this century soars like Jesus
The devils in the deeps look up and say they see a
Nimitation of Simon Magus in Judea
Craft by name by nature craft they cry
About the pretty flyer the angels fly
Enoch Elijah Apollonius of Tyana hover
With Icarus round the first airworthy ever
For those whom the Eucharist transports they now and
    then make way
Host-elevating priests ascending endlessly
The aeroplane alights at last with outstretched pinions
Then the sky is filled with swallows in their millions
The rooks come flocking the owls the hawks
Flamingoes from Africa and ibises and storks
The roc bird famed in song and story soars
With Adam's skull the first head in its claws
The eagle stoops screaming from heaven's verge
From America comes the little humming-bird
From China the long and supple
One-winged peehees that fly in couples
Behold the dove spirit without alloy
That ocellate peacock and lyre-bird convoy
The phoenix flame-devoured flame-revived

Un instant voile tout de son ardente cendre
Les sirènes laissant les périlleux détroits
Arrivent en chantant bellement toutes trois
Et tous aigle phénix et pihis de la Chine
Fraternisent avec la volante machine

Maintenant tu marches dans Paris tout seul parmi la foule
Des troupeaux d'autobus mugissants près de toi roulent
L'angoisse de l'amour te serre le gosier
Comme si tu ne devais jamais plus être aimé
Si tu vivais dans l'ancien temps tu entrerais dans un
    monastère
Vous avez honte quand vous vous surprenez à dire une
    prière
Tu te moques de toi et comme le feu de l'Enfer ton rire
    pétille
Les étincelles de ton rire dorent le fond de ta vie
C'est un tableau pendu dans un sombre musée
Et quelquefois tu vas le regarder de près

Aujourd'hui tu marches dans Paris les femmes sont
    ensanglantées
C'était et je voudrais ne pas m'en souvenir c'était au
    déclin de la beauté

Entourée de flammes ferventes Notre-Dame m'a regardé
    à Chartres
Le sang de votre Sacré Cœur m'a inondé à Montmartre
Je suis malade d'ouïr les paroles bienheureuses
L'amour dont je souffre est une maladie honteuse
Et l'image qui te possède te fait survivre dans l'insomnie
    et dans l'angoisse
C'est toujours près de toi cette image qui passe

All with its ardent ash an instant hides
Leaving the perilous straits the sirens three
Divinely singing join the company
And eagle phoenix peehees fraternize
One and all with the machine that flies

Now you walk in Paris alone among the crowd
Herds of bellowing buses hemming you about
Anguish of love parching you within
As though you were never to be loved again
If you lived in olden times you would get you to a cloister
You are ashamed when you catch yourself at a paternoster
You are your own mocker and like hellfire your laughter
    crackles
Golden on your life's hearth fall the sparks of your laughter
It is a picture in a dark museum hung
And you sometimes go and contemplate it long

To-day you walk in Paris the women are blood-red
It was and would I could forget it was at beauty's ebb

From the midst of fervent flames Our Lady beheld me
    at Chartres
The blood of your Sacred Heart flooded me in Montmartre
I am sick with hearing the words of bliss
The love I endure is like a syphilis
And the image that possesses you and never leaves your
    side
In anguish and insomnia keeps you alive

Maintenant tu es au bord de la Méditerranée
Sous les citronniers qui sont en fleur toute l'année
Avec tes amis tu te promènes en barque
L'un est Nissard il y a un Mentonasque et deux
   Turbiasques
Nous regardons avec effroi les poulpes des profondeurs
Et parmi les algues nagent les poissons images du Sauveur

Tu es dans le jardin d'une auberge aux environs de Prague
Tu te sens tout heureux une rose est sur la table
Et tu observes au lieu d'écrire ton conte en prose
La cétoine qui dort dans le cœur de la rose

Épouvanté tu te vois dessiné dans les agates de Saint-Vit
Tu étais triste à mourir le jour où tu t'y vis
Tu ressembles au Lazare affolé par le jour
Les aiguilles de l'horloge du quartier juif vont à rebours
Et tu recules aussi dans ta vie lentement
En montant au Hradchin et le soir en écoutant
Dans les tavernes chanter des chansons tchèques

Te voici à Marseille au milieu des pastèques

Te voici à Coblence à l'hôtel du Géant

Te voici à Rome assis sous un néflier du Japon

Te voici à Amsterdam avec une jeune fille que tu trouves
   belle et qui est laide
Elle doit se marier avec un étudiant de Leyde

Now you are on the Riviera among
The lemon-trees that flower all year long
With your friends you go for a sail on the sea
One is from Nice one from Menton and two from La Turbie
The octopuses in the depths fill us with horror
And in the seaweed fishes swim emblems of the Saviour

You are in an inn-garden near Prague
You feel perfectly happy a rose is on the table
And you observe instead of writing your story in prose
The chafer asleep in the heart of the rose

Appalled you see your image in the agates of Saint Vitus
That day you were fit to die with sadness
You look like Lazarus frantic in the daylight
The hands of the clock in the Jewish quarter go to left
    from right
And you too live slowly backwards
Climbing up to the Hradchin or listening as night falls
To Czech songs being sung in taverns

Here you are in Marseilles among the water-melons

Here you are in Coblenz at the Giant's Hostelry

Here you are in Rome under a Japanese medlar-tree

Here you are in Amsterdam with an ill-favoured maiden
You find her beautiful she is engaged to a student in
    Leyden

On y loue des chambres en latin Cubicula locanda
Je m'en souviens j'y ai passé trois jours et autant à Gouda

Tu es à Paris chez le juge d'instruction
Comme un criminel on te met en état d'arrestation

Tu as fait de douloureux et de joyeux voyages
Avant de t'apercevoir du mensonge et de l'âge
Tu as souffert de l'amour à vingt et à trente ans
J'ai vécu comme un fou et j'ai perdu mon temps
Tu n'oses plus regarder tes mains et à tous moments
    je voudrais sangloter
Sur toi sur celle que j'aime sur tout ce qui t'a épouvanté

Tu regardes les yeux pleins de larmes ces pauvres émigrants
Ils croient en Dieu ils prient les femmes allaitent des enfants
Ils emplissent de leur odeur le hall de la gare Saint-Lazare
Ils ont foi dans leur étoile comme les rois-mages
Ils espèrent gagner de l'argent dans l'Argentine
Et revenir dans leur pays après avoir fait fortune
Une famille transporte un édredon rouge comme vous
    transportez votre cœur
Cet édredon et nos rêves sont aussi irréels
Quelques-uns de ces émigrants restent ici et se logent
Rue des Rosiers ou rue des Écouffes dans des bouges
Je les ai vus souvent le soir ils prennent l'air dans la rue
Et se déplacent rarement comme les pièces aux échecs
Il y a surtout des Juifs leurs femmes portent perruque
Elles restent assises exsangues au fond des boutiques

There they let their rooms in Latin cubicula locanda
I remember I spent three days there and as many in Gouda

You are in Paris with the examining magistrate
They clap you in gaol like a common reprobate

Grievous and joyous voyages you made
Before you knew what falsehood was and age
At twenty you suffered from love and at thirty again
My life was folly and my days in vain
You dare not look at your hands tears haunt my eyes
For you for her I love and all the old miseries

Weeping you watch the wretched emigrants
They believe in God they pray the women suckle their
    infants
They fill with their smell the station of Saint-Lazare
Like the wise men from the East they have faith in their star
They hope to prosper in the Argentine
And to come home having made their fortune
A family transports a red eiderdown as you your heart
An eiderdown as unreal as our dreams
Some go no further doss in the stews
Of the Rue des Rosiers or the Rue des Écouffes
Often in the streets I have seen them in the gloaming
Taking the air and like chessmen seldom moving
They are mostly Jews the wives wear wigs and in
The depths of shadowy dens bloodless sit on and on

Tu es debout devant le zinc d'un bar crapuleux
Tu prends un café à deux sous parmi les malheureux

Tu es la nuit dans un grand restaurant

Ces femmes ne sont pas méchantes elles ont des soucis
    cependant
Toutes même la plus laide a fait souffrir son amant

Elle est la fille d'un sergent de ville de Jersey

Ses mains que je n'avais pas vues sont dures et gercées

J'ai une pitié immense pour les coutures de son ventre

J'humilie maintenant à une pauvre fille au rire horrible
    ma bouche

Tu es seul le matin va venir
Les laitiers font tinter leurs bidons dans les rues

La nuit s'éloigne ainsi qu'une belle Métive
C'est Ferdine la fausse ou Léa l'attentive

Et tu bois cet alcool brûlant comme ta vie
Ta vie que tu bois comme une eau-de-vie

You stand at the bar of a crapulous café
Drinking coffee at two sous a time in the midst of the
  unhappy

It is night you are in a restaurant it is superior

These women are decent enough they have their troubles
  however
All even the ugliest one have made their lovers suffer

She is a Jersey police-constable's daughter

Her hands I had not seen are chapped and hard

The seams of her belly go to my heart

To a poor harlot horribly laughing I humble my mouth

You are alone morning is at hand
In the streets the milkmen rattle their cans

Like a dark beauty night withdraws
Watchful Leah or Ferdine the false

And you drink this alcohol burning like your life
Your life that you drink like spirit of wine

Tu marches vers Auteuil tu veux aller chez toi à pied
Dormir parmi tes fétiches d'Océanie et de Guinée
Ils sont des Christ d'une autre forme et d'une autre
   croyance
Ce sont les Christ inférieurs des obscures espérances

Adieu Adieu

Soleil cou coupé

You walk towards Auteuil you want to walk home and
    sleep
Among your fetishes from Guinea and the South Seas
Christs of another creed another guise
The lowly Christs of dim expectancies

Adieu Adieu

Sun corseless head

SÉBASTIEN CHAMFORT

Huit Maximes

Le sot qui a un moment d'esprit étonne et scandalise comme
des chevaux de fiacre qui galopent.

Long after Chamfort

Wit in fools has something shocking
Like cabhorses galloping.

Le théâtre tragique a le grand inconvénient moral de mettre trop d'importance à la vie et à la mort.

The trouble with tragedy is the fuss it makes
About life and death and other tuppenny aches.

Quand on soutient que les gens les moins sensibles sont, à tout prendre, les plus heureux, je me rappelle le proverbe indien: 'Il vaut mieux être assis que debout, couché qu'assis, mort que tout cela.'

Better on your arse than on your feet,
Flat on your back than either, dead than the lot.

Quand on a été bien tourmenté, bien fatigué par sa propre sensibilité, on s'aperçoit qu'il faut vivre au jour le jour, oublier beaucoup, enfin éponger la vie à mesure qu'elle s'écoule.

Live and clean forget from day to day,
Mop life up as fast as it dribbles away.

La pensée console de tout et remédie à tout. Si quelquefois elle vous fait du mal, demandez-lui le remède du mal qu'elle vous a fait, elle vous le donnera.

Ask of all-healing, all-consoling thought
Salve and solace for the woe it wrought.

L'espérance n'est qu'un charlatan qui nous trompe sans cesse; et, pour moi, le bonheur n'a commencé que lorsque je l'ai eu perdu. Je mettrais volontiers sur la porte du paradis le vers que le Dante a mis sur celle de l'enfer: *Lasciate ogni speranza etc.*

Hope is a knave befools us evermore,
Which till I lost no happiness was mine.
I strike from hell's to grave on heaven's door:
All hope abandon ye who enter in.

Vivre est une maladie dont le sommeil nous soulage toutes les seize heures. C'est un palliatif; la mort est le remède.

sleep till death
healeth
come ease
this life disease

Que le cœur de l'homme est creux et plein d'ordure.

how hollow heart and full
of filth thou art

Tailpiece

who may tell the tale
of the old man?
weigh absence in a scale?
mete want with a span?
the sum assess
of the world's woes?
nothingness
in words enclose?

Translations of Beckett's untranslated French poems

to be there without jaws without teeth [p. 42]

to be there without jaws without teeth / where the pleasure of losing
flees / along with that scarcely inferior / of winning / and Roscelin
and waiting / adverb oh little gift / void void if not for tatters of songs
/ *mon père m'a donné un mari* / or bunching your fingers / waiting for
her to moisten / so much that she'll crave until the elegiac / hobnailed
clogs still far from Les Halles / or the rabble's water groaning in the
pipes / or no more sound / waiting for her to moisten since that's how
it is / get the rest over with / and come / to the idiot mouth to the
creeping hand / to the basement door to the eye that listens / for the
far-off motion of silver scissors

Ascension [p. 43]

through the thin partition / this day when a child / prodigal in its own
way / returned to its family / I hear the voice / it is excited it is
commenting / on the football world cup // always too young // at
the same time through the open window / in brief through the air /
mutely / the swell of the faithful // her blood spurted in abun-
dance / on the sheets on the sweetpea on her bloke / with his
revolting fingers he closed the lids / on her large green aston-
ished eyes // she wanders nimble / on my tomb of air

The Fly [p. 44]

between the scene and me / the window / empty besides // belly to
the ground / girthed in its black guts / panicked antennae
joined wings / hooked legs mouth sucking the void / slicing
the azure crashing against the invisible / under my impotent
thumb it makes / the sea and the peaceful sky capsize

so it's no use [p. 45]

so it's no use / through good times and bad / imprisoned at home
imprisoned abroad / as if it were yesterday remember the mammoth /
the dinothere the first kisses / the glacial periods bringing nothing
new / the great heat of the thirteenth of their era / Kant hunched
coldly over smoking Lisbon / to dream in generations of oak and
forget one's father / his eyes whether he wore a moustache / if he was
kind what he died of / it won't stop eating you for want of appetite /
through bad times and worse / imprisoned at home imprisoned
abroad

Rue de Vaugirard [p. 47]

halfway along / I release the button and beaming with candour / expose
the plate to the light and shadow / then set off again fortified / by an
unimpeachable negative

Lutetian Amphitheatre [p. 48]

From where we are sitting above the tiers / I see us enter from the
rue des Arènes side, / hesitate, look up in the air, then heavily / come
towards us across the dark sand, / uglier and uglier, as ugly as the
others, / but mute. A little green dog / enters running from the rue
Monge side, / she stops, she follows him with her eyes, / he crosses
the arena, he disappears / behind the pedestal of the savant Gabriel
de Mortillet. / She turns back, I have left, I climb the rustic steps /
alone, I touch with my left hand / the rustic ramp, it's made of
concrete. She hesitates, / takes a step towards the rue Monge exit,
then follows me. / I shiver, it is myself I rejoin, / it is with other eyes
that I now look / at the sand, the puddles under the drizzle, / a little
girl trailing a hoop behind her, / a couple, lovers perhaps, hand in
hand, / the empty tiers, the tall houses, the sky / that shines on us too
late. / I turn around, amazed / to find his sad face there.

So what if there is a land [p. 53]

So what if there is a land / where forgetfulness where forgetfulness weighs / sweetly on the unnamed worlds / there the head is silenced the head is mute / and you know no you know nothing / the song of dead mouths dies / on the shore it ends its journey / there is no cause to mourn // my solitude I know it ok I know it badly / I've got time I tell myself I've got time / but what weather famished bone filthy weather / a sky forever growing paler my grain of sky / the ray that climbs ocellate trembling / the microns of dark years // you want me to go from A to B I cannot / I cannot come out I am in a trackless land / yes yes it's a fine thing you have there a very fine thing / what is that ask me no more questions / spiral dust of instants what is this the same / calm love hate calm calm

Death of A.D. [p. 54]

and there to be there still there / pressed against my old poxed plank of dark / days and nights blindly crushed / to be there and not fleeing fleeing and being there / bent towards the confession of time dying / of having been what it was done what it did / to me to my friend dead yesterday gleaming eye / long teeth panting in his beard devouring / the lives of the saints a life per day of life / reliving its black sins at night / dead yesterday while I lived / and to be there drinking above the storm / the burden of irremissible time / clutching the old wood witness to departures / witness to returns

long live dead my only season [p. 55]

long live dead my only season / white lilies chrysanthemums / lively nests abandoned / mud of April leaves / fine grey days of frost

mirlitonnades [pps. 69–105]

facing / the worst / laugh / till you burst

   *

back home / at night / on with the light // extinguish see / the night see / pressed to the window / the face

   *

all said and done / game over amounts / to a quarter billion / quarter
hours gone / not including / extra time

    *

far end of void / after what watch / eye thought it saw / the head
feebly stir / calmed him saying / all in the head

    *

silence such that what / once was will never again / be torn by the
murmur / of a word with no past / helpless not to say too much / just
saying I'll go on

    *

listen to them / add up / words / upon words / without a word / step /
upon step / one by / one

    *

flashes edgings / of the shuttle / take more than a step fade / about-
turn shine like new // halt rather / far from each / by your self
selfless / out of their reach

    *

surmise if this / should one day this / one fine day / surmise / if one
day / one fine day this / should cease / surmise

    *

first off / flat on the rough / right / or left / no matter // then / flat on
the right / or the left / the left / or the right // at last / flat on the left /
or the right / no matter / on the lot / the head

    *

flux the cause / that each thing / busy being / each thing / say this
here / this here even / busy being / is busy not / talk
about it

    *

saturday respite / no more laughter / from midnight / to midnight /
and no tears after

    *

each day the desire / one day to be alive / not of course without scorn / for one day having been born

*

night which makes / us pray for dawn / night of grace / come down

*

nothing no one / will have been / in vain / so long as / nothing no one / been

*

best foot no sooner forward / for the last step / than rests
waiting / as custom dictates / for the other do likewise / as custom
dictates / and so bears the burden / further on / as custom dictates /
thus far at least

*

whatever good / ill seen by the eyes / the thread tired / hands have
dropped / hold on tight / fingers and eyes / the good comes back / as
better

*

whatever ill / the heart has known / whatever curses / the head rained
down / on itself / recall / the worst comes back / as worse

*

don't miss when in Tangier / the Saint-André graveyard where / under
stone the dead are laid / itself by flowers buried / a seat to honour /
Arthur Keyser / with him in spirit who / sits a while up here below

*

further on one marks where / Caroline Hay Taylor lies / to her belief
stayed true / that hope must spring from life / departed Ireland for
paradise / in August nineteen thirty-two

*

don't miss when in Stuttgart / the long rue Neckar / the call of the
void / not itself any more / so strong is the feeling / you've been here
before

*

old going / old halts // going / absent / absent / halt

*

fools who said / never again / quick / say it again

*

step by step / nowhere / none alone / knows how / little steps /
nowhere / stubbornly

*

dream / without cease / nor ever / peace

*

dead among / her dead flies / the spider rocked / by a gentle breeze

*

whence / the voice that says / live // another life

*

words that survive / life / keep him company / still a while

*

rivers and oceans / left him for living / at the Courtablon burn / near
the Mare-Chaudron

*

resolutely / past all care / passes himself out / going nowhere

*

venturing from his hermit's refuge / it was the calm after the deluge

*

no sooner heard himself unleash / the words all over than / his life at
last began to flash / its toothy grin at him

*

the night come when at last / his soul was to be repossessed / incontinent buffoon / he let it go an hour too soon

*

no more / memories all told than aged / one day in April / one day
old

    ★

his shadow one night / came in from the cold / lengthened turned
white / dissolved

    ★

dark sister / who art in hell / laying about you / everywhere / what are
you waiting for

    ★

the final murmur / of a dwarf in his ninetieth year / grant me for pity
/ a full-sized bier

    ★

all out of dreams a buckhare / tired of the hunt constrained / to quit
its den made sure to leave / the candlestick behind

'Whoroscope'. First published by Nancy Cunard's Hours Press in Paris, 1930. Beckett's notes, like Eliot's to *The Waste Land*, were added at his publisher's request, and draw on his reading of Baillet's *La vie de Monsieur Descartes* and John Pentland Mahaffy's *Descartes* (1880).

'Gnome'. Written after Beckett's resignation and flight from Trinity College, Dublin in January 1932; first published *Dublin Magazine* July–September 1934. The title connects the Greek 'gnosis' (knowledge) with the idea of a diminished being. According to Beckett, the poem was inspired by Goethe's 'Xenien' (Xenia: gifts to the departing). Originally, and until 1977, 'a' in l. 3 read 'the'.

'The Vulture'. First published in *Echo's Bones and Other Precipitates* (1935). Beckett acknowledged a debt to Goethe's 'Harzreise im Winter'.

'Enueg I'. *Echo's Bones*. The 'enueg' (= *ennui*) is a Provençal genre of stylised complaint. The Dublin suburb Chapelizod is the setting for Joyce's *Finnegans Wake* and is celebrated in myth as the burial place of Iseult of Ireland. Nepenthe is a drug of forgetfulness, and moly a herb used by Odysseus as a charm against Circe's enchantments. The concluding four lines derive from Rimbaud's 'Barbare'.

'Enueg II'. *Echo's Bones*. Veronica mopped Christ's brow with a sudarium: 'veronica mundi' is a Veronica 'of the world', and 'veronica munda' a 'pure' Veronica. Deirdre Bair describes Beckett storming out of painter Sean O'Sullivan's studio, decrying another artist as 'a Veronicist who would wipe the face of Christ with a sanitary towel'. The German 'doch' is used to contradict a negative statement; in Beckett's notebooks for the abandoned play *Human Wishes*, the phrase 'Dr J in love' is annotated 'Doch' in the margin, while elsewhere Beckett notes Johnson's habit of saying 'No, sir' when he wished to express agreement. 'Feet in marmalade' derives from an expression of Beckett's friend Georges Pelorson's grandmother.

'Alba'. *Dublin Magazine* VI October–December 1931, then *Echo's Bones*. A Provençal song of the dawn, lamenting the separation of the poet from the beloved. The areca is an Asian palm tree.

'Dortmunder'. *Echo's Bones*. The title refers to a German beer. A plagal, unlike a perfect cadence, offers no resolution from leading note to tonic. The k'în is a

Chinese lute. Habakkuk (*sic*) is unique among biblical prophets for openly questioning the ways of God.

'Sanies I'. *Echo's Bones*. A sanies is a seropurulent discharge from an infection. Portrane, in north Co. Dublin, features in the short story 'Fingal', where Jonathan Swift is described as having imprisoned his 'motte' (girlfriend) there. A potwalloper is one who claimed a vote on the basis on having boiled (walloped) a kettle in the parish for six consecutive months; with its franchise vested in 'potwallopers', Swords was historically one of the few free (though notoriously corrupt) boroughs in Ireland, its name recalling another Latin word for filth, *sordes*. Holles Street: site of a Dublin maternity hospital.

'Sanies II'. *Echo's Bones*. Gracieuse, Percinet and Belle-Belle are characters from the Comtesse d'Aulnoy's fairy tales. The Latin line (from Plautus) means 'dead bullocks strike against living women'. The closing fantasy of flagellation prompts thoughts of the Dublin madam Becky Cooper, whose establishment featured a reproduction of Henry Holiday's 'Dante and Beatrice'.

'Serena I.' *Echo's Bones*. A Provençal song of evening, longing for night, and for the beloved. A version of the poem sent to Thomas MacGreevy with a letter of 8 October 1932 features an additional opening stanza. Pietro Aretino and Daniel Defoe both castigated urban decadence. Wren's 'giant bully' is Sir Christopher Wren's memorial to the victims of the great fire of 1666.

'Serena II'. *Echo's Bones*. The poet's Kerry Blue bitch revisits the Irish west coast in a dream before whelping in a bog. Croagh Patrick is a site of pilgrimage in Co. Mayo.

'Serena III'. *Echo's Bones*. 'Pothook of beauty': William Hogarth espoused the sigmoid line, as encountered by the poet in the decorations of the Merrion Flats. Misery Hill was once a leper colony and site of public executions.

'Malacoda'. *Echo's Bones*. Malacoda is among the devils in *Inferno* XX who threaten Dante and Virgil, and breaks wind at them. His latter-day incarnation, an undertaker kneeling by the coffin of the poet's father, is similarly flatulent. A Jan van Huysum painting in the National Gallery, London, features a butterfly (the 'imago' 'on the box').

'Da Tagte Es'. *Echo's Bones*. The title may derive from the *minnesinger* Walther von der Vogelweide's 'dô taget ez und muos ich waken' ('it dawns and I must waken'), though Beckett's notes suggest Heinrich von Morungen as another possible source.

'Echo's Bones'. *Echo's Bones*. In Ovid's *Metamorphoses*, Echo mourns for the dead Narcissus and wastes away to stone. 'Gantelope' is an archaic form of 'gauntlet' (running the gauntlet), which contains the after-image of an antelope.

'Yoke of Liberty'. *European Caravan*, part 1 (New York, 1931). Originally 'Moly'.

'Antipepsis'. *Metre* 3 Autumn 1997. Possibly written in response to the banning of *More Pricks Than Kicks* in Ireland (1934), despite the handwritten addition 'After Saint Lô 1946' (Beckett International Foundation, University of Reading [UoR] typescript). 'Ochone' is a Gaelic term of lament. L.8 originally 'The ass was the more intelligent', 'ass' crossed out and amended to 'cart'.

'Cascando'. Composed 1936; first published *Dublin Magazine* XI October–December 1936. A musical term denoting decreased volume and a slower tempo.

'Ooftish'. Composed 1937; first published *Transition* 27 (April–May 1938). Originally titled 'Whiting'. 'Ooftish' derives from a Yiddish expression, meaning to lay one's cash on the table.

'*elles viennent*'/'they come'. Composed 25 January 1938; first published (French text only) *Temps modernes* 14 November 1946, one of twelve poems published there. The English text first appeared in Peggy Guggenheim's *Out of This Century* (1946).

'*être là sans mâchoires sans dents*'. Composed 1937–9; first published *Temps modernes* 1946. The medieval thinker Roscellinus Compendiensis denied the existence of universals. The image of the Fates cutting the thread of life recurs at the end of the *mirlitonnades*.

'Ascension'. Composed 1938; first published *Temps modernes* 1946. The football world cup took place in Paris in 1938. An alternative final couplet occurs in the version Beckett sent MacGreevy on 15 June 1938: '*en reçoit-il une colombe /aussi souvent que moi*'.

'*La Mouche*'. Composed 1938; first published *Temps modernes* 1946.

'*ainsi a-t-on beau*'. Composed 1937–9; first published *Temps modernes* 1946. Immanuel Kant wrote prolifically on the Lisbon earthquake of 1755.

'Dieppe'. Composed in French in 1937 and published in *Temps modernes* (French text only). English text first published in the *Irish Times* 9 June 1945, where 'lights of old' read 'lighted town'. Originates in Hölderlin's 'Der Spaziergang'.

'Rue de Vaugirard'. Composed 1937–9. *Temps modernes* 1946. A thoroughfare near Beckett's apartment on the rue des Favorites.

'Arènes de Lutèce'. *Temps modernes*. Lutetia was the Roman name for Paris. The Roman amphitheatre is in the fifth arrondissement. Gabriel de Mortillet

(1821–1898) was a French palaeontologist; evidence of Beckett's interest in palaeontology at this time can be found in the *Whoroscope* notebook (University of Reading [UoR]).

'Saint-Lô'. First published in the *Irish Times* 24 June 1946, where l.3 was originally two lines: 'and the old mind / ghost-abandoned'; revised for *Poems in English* (1961).The River Vire flows through Saint-Lô, a town in Lower Normandy where Beckett worked for the Red Cross after the war, as described in his radio talk 'The Capital of the Ruins'.

'*bon bon il est un pays*'. Composed February 1947; first published *Cahiers des saisons* 2 October 1955, one of a group of three poems, where it is titled '*Accul*'. A rare example in the Beckett canon of a commissioned text, written at the request of Geer van Velde.

'*Mort de A.D*'. Composed after the death of Arthur Darley ('A.D.'), 30 December 1948; first published *Cahiers des saisons* 1955. Darley, a colleague of Beckett's at Saint-Lô in Normandy, also features in his final prose work, *Stirrings Still*.

'*vive morte ma seule saison*'. Composed 1947–9; first published *Cahiers des saisons* 1955.

'*je suis ce cours de sable qui glisse*'/'my way is in the sand flowing'. Reportedly written by Beckett on Killiney Strand, Co. Dublin, during a summer visit to his mother in 1948; French and English versions first published *Transition Forty-Eight* 2 (June 1948).

'*que ferais-je sans ce monde sans visage sans questions*'/ 'what would I do without this world'. Composed 1948; first published *Transition Forty-Eight* 2 (June 1948). Line 10 originally '*comme hier comme avant-hier*'.

'*je voudrais que mon amour meure*'/'I would like my love to die'. Composed 1948; first published *Transition Forty-Eight* 2 (June 1948). French text originally *et dans les rues* (l. 3) and *pleurant la seule qui m'ait aimé* (l. 4), and English text (l. 4) originally 'mourning the first and last to love me'.

'Song'. From the play *Words and Music*, first published in *Evergreen Review* (1962).

'*hors crâne seul dedans*'. Composed 1–4 January 1974; first published *Minuit* 21 (November 1976). Bocca degli Alberti was a traitor, encased in ice in the ninth circle of hell (*Inferno* XXXII). 'Something there' freely translates this French poem.

'Something there'. Composed 1–4 January 1974; first published *New Departures* 7/8 and 9/10 (August 1975).

'dread nay'. Composed 1974; first published *Collected Poems* (1977). The chattering sound made by the stork can also be found in *Inferno* XXXII.

'Roundelay'. Composed July 1976; first published *Modern Drama* 19 (September 1976).

'*mirlitonnades*'. *Poèmes, suivi de mirlitonnades* (Minuit, 1978). The make-up of the sequence varies from edition to edition of Beckett's poetry; this printing follows the original text. After this publication Beckett continued to write new poems in French and English in the *sottisier* notebook. Manuscripts in Trinity College, Dublin describe poems written in the late 1980s as '*mirlitonnades*', making a case for all his short late poems to be seen as implicit additions to the sequence. A *mirliton* is a kazoo, and *mirlitonnades* doggerel verse in which to wrap the instrument. The Mare-Chaudron and rue de Courtablon are places in Ussy, whither Beckett retreated from Paris and did much of his writing in later life. The dark sister of '*noire sœur*' is Atropos (cf. note to '*être là sans mâchoires sans dents*'). The hare of '*à bout de songes un bouquin*' derives from La Fontaine's '*Le Lièvre et les grenouilles*'.

'one dead of night'. Composed June 1977; first published *Poetry Review* 86:3 1996.

'there', 'again gone'. Composed 1981; first published (together with a third, 'head on hands') under the single title 'pss' in *New Departures* 14 (1982), but recourse to the *sottisier* notebook clarifies that they are separate poems. 'there' answers Petruchio's question in *The Taming of the Shrew*: 'Where is the life that late I led?'

'bail bail till better/founder'. Composed 11 April 1981 (UoR *sottisier* notebook).

'Là'. Composed 19 January 1987; first published *Journal of Beckett Studies* [*JOBS*] 1.1 and 2 1992, where it carried a dedication 'For Jim' (James Knowlson).

'Go where never before'. Composed 24 January 1987; English version of 'Là', first published together in *JOBS* 1.1 and 2 1992.

'Brief Dream'. Composed November 1987; first published *JOBS* 1.1 and 2 1992.

Comment dire/what is the word. French text dated 29 October 1988, English text 23 April 1989. Composed 1988; first published *Libération* 1 June 1989 ('*Comment dire*') and *Sunday Correspondent* 31 December 1989 ('what is the word'). 'what is the word' was Beckett's last piece of writing.

Translations

'Delta'. *This Quarter* 2.4 April–May–June 1930. Eugenio Montale (1896–1981), Italian poet, Nobel Prize for Literature 1975.

'Louis Armstrong'. From Nancy Cunard's *Negro, An Anthology* (1934). Ernst Moerman (1897–1944), Belgian author and film director.

'Drunken Boat'. Whiteknights Press (Reading, 1976). Arthur Rimbaud (1854–1891), French poet. Beckett offered the translation to *This Quarter* in 1932, but the journal ceased publication shortly afterwards. The text was believed lost for decades before resurfacing in 1975; it was first published in a limited edition the following year.

'Lady Love', 'Out of Sight in the Direction of My Body'. First published in *Thorns of Thunder: Selected Poems of Paul Éluard* (London, 1936). Paul Éluard (1895–1952), French surrealist poet.

'Zone'. *Transition Fifty* 6 (October 1950), reprinted by Dolmen Press (1972). Guillaume Apollinaire (1880–1918), Polish-born French surrealist poet.

'Long after Chamfort'. First published *The Blue Guitar* December 1975 (maxims 1–6), *Hermathena* CXV 1973 (number 6), and *Collected Poems* (numbers 7 and 8). Nicolas-Sébastien Chamfort (1741–1794), mordant French aphorist. The last of the eight maxims derives not from Chamfort but from Pascal.

'Tailpiece'. From *Watt*, and placed last in all previous editions of Beckett's poetry.